Il0863960

If All Else Fails ...
Laugh!

Suzie Humphreys

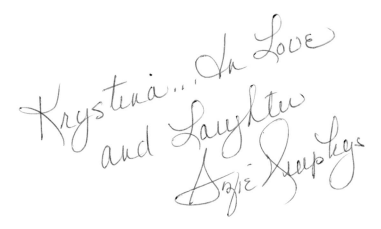

Krystina ... In Love
and Laughter
Suzie Humphreys

Tivydale Press
Fredericksburg, Texas

Copyright © 2005 by Suzie Humphreys
All rights reserved
Printed in U.S.A.
Library of Congress Control Number 2006902032
ISBN 0-9777906-0-6

Cover design by Kim McLaughlin
Text design by Sheryl Mehary
Cover photograph by Constance Ashley

This book may not be reproduced in whole or in
part, by electronic or any other means which exist or
may yet be developed, without permission of:

Tivydale Press
12686 FM 2093
Fredericksburg, Texas 78624

Dedication

*To The Mayo's ... my husband Tom, our
son Joshua, my stepchildren Mike,
Catherine, Cynthia, Diane, and Susan
(whom we all miss every day), my brother
in law Maxey, and his wife Frances.
All welcomed this only child into their
circle of acceptance, good humor and love.
Step families are a gift.*

Acknowledgements

Once this book was an idea floating in my mind. I had talked about this idea to friends and family, but it just remained an idea. Then a first story came to mind, an incident that I felt was worth remembering, so I sat down at the computer and wrote it out. Through two years, I sat down at the computer and wrote other stories. The "idea" of the book had grown into an actual project. Still, I had no idea of it's outcome or where to go from there. Then, one day the phone rang. It was Thorn Bacon of Best Seller Consultants. He said "Suzie, I've heard your CD and YOU HAVE A BOOK IN YOU."

To Thorn Bacon and his wife Ursula, for motivating me and carrying the book from the computer to completion. To Dedie Leahy of Dedie Leahy and Company, my friend and encourager, who early on rendered her help in the project. To my fabulous friend and photographer, Constance Ashley, who, even on my worst day, can take a photograph of me that I like. To Kim McLaughlin for her upbeat cover design and Sheryl Mehary for patiently revising the text. To Tom Mayo, my closest critic, who gave me endless encouragement and praise and making me feel that there was something in these pages that people will want to read. To you, the reader, oh how I hope you feel that you didn't waste your money.

Contents

Preface

There is nothing spectacular about me or my life, though there is nothing ordinary either. My life and I fall somewhere in between. It is in this "in between" where most of us live. To this end, perhaps you will find some connection or comfort in the events written about in this book. Actually, I don't think of them as stories, but rather as little miracles. Because even though the characters are real and the incidents actually did happen, they seem to me to be almost mystical messages — some secret way of getting me to understand the point of the story. Seeing the "point" is what I call a little miracle. My book is about some of those miracles that have happened to me, sometimes even in the face of hope or hopelessness, and in my everyday encounters with people who have come and gone in my life.

Perhaps you and I traveled a thousand miles of railroad track, beginning one misty day at dawn. We might have been on the same yellow school bus the morning we started our first trip to summer camp. We could have planned the second grade Halloween party together in carpool line, or stretched our muscles in the same exercise class the one time I went. Perhaps we never met at all, until now. But we are on this journey together and I am happy to be sharing some of mine with you.

Suzie Humphreys

Introduction

I have no memory of my mother and father ever living together before their divorce. My memories as a child revolve mostly around my mother; although my father picked me up at school every day of my life from the first through the twelfth grade. He never missed a day. He never missed Christmas morning or a birthday, and there were the weekends of hunting or fishing, and trips to the park. But it was to my mother to whom my life was glued. My five feet, one inch mother was bigger than life to me then and she is even larger now that I am older and have given up my petty resentments.

I visited her last week and while we were going through her jewelry and talking about its history and its value, she said quite matter-of-factly, "I'm not going to live much longer."

I suppose I tried to maintain some sort of matter-of-fact attitude. I didn't try to talk her out of her decision, for I had been thinking that she was more frail and stooped over. Her eyesight was growing worse every day. But then what can you expect when you are ninety? She was still mobile, on a walker. She cooked for herself and, though it took her longer, the food was every bit as tasty as always. I mean what can you expect? When my mother was forty she never thought she would live to see fifty!

We had finished looking at the treasures and changed the dying subject, when she hoisted herself up by her walker and hobbled over to the small Wurlitzer piano sitting upright against the wall. She carefully sat down and placed her tiny feet on the peddles, positioned her hands above the keyboard, and in less than the count of three, began to play one of her favorites, a perky and spirited rendition of

Alexander's Ragtime Band. As I watched her hips swivel to the beat and her body bounce to the rhythm, I was transported back to the beginning, as I remember, of the first time I ever heard her play.

We were a pair, we were! The precocious five year old with the red hair and the small beautiful woman with the hour glass figure, Betty Grable legs, and the incredible personality. For a time we rented a room. Then, as my mother began to become more successful, we finally took a one-bedroom apartment. It was then that she bought the most precious thing she wanted … a piano.

While she sold insurance in the evening, I was dropped off at the Broadway Theatre where I would usually sit through one movie twice and eat three boxes of popcorn. Sometimes my mom would slip into the chair beside me and together we would watch the last twenty minutes of the film. When we got home, she unlocked the door, dropped her purse on the chair and, without ever turning on a light, sat down at the piano and played the song she had heard in the movie. She called it playing by ear. Her fingers would glide across the keyboard and she didn't even watch them. I marveled at that and when I was alone I sat at the piano with my small hands bent over the keyboard and *waited* for my fingers to fly across the ivories. Nothing ever happened! I took up singing instead.

My mother taught me to harmonize with her to "Carolina in the Morning." When we reached the part that went "strolling with my girlie when the dew is pearlie early in the morning," we always rolled our eyes at each other and smiled the biggest smiles our faces would hold. Not only was unspoken encouragement in her eyes, but the purest expression of joy on her face showed me that I was doing something pleasing. That was my first introduction to "pride." It was also my first introduction to "playing to the crowd."

From that time on, I was never content to sit in the audience. I always wanted to be in front of them. I loved the feeling that came from looking in their faces and connecting with an emotion of humor or joy or sadness. The pleasure that came to me when I was five, as an unconscious gift from my mother, was the response I looked for in everything I did. I wasn't aware of it then, and I did not define it until some sixty-two years later when I watched her play as if she had never gotten up from the piano bench.

Her spirit was exactly the same. Time and disappointment had not diminished or extinguished it. She had never given way to complaining or small thinking. Robert Hastings, in his wonderfully written prose entitled "The Station" expressed it this way:

It isn't the burdens of today that drive men mad. It's the regrets over yesterday
And the fear of tomorrow. Regret and fear are twin "thieves" that rob us of today.

Perhaps that is the most amazing gift my mother passed down to me — to take the "licks" in life and not be beaten by them. There it is! My first introduction to Attitude, the positive kind. To make mistakes and not agonize over them; to know that there is no such thing as a wrong decision. Every decision leads to a lesson. Whether or not we learn it, is one thing. Whether of not we even look for the lesson is something else!

I believe there is a lesson in every encounter, pleasant or unpleasant; in every relationship, a minute long or a lifetime; in every choice selfishly made or selflessly chosen.

The point ... the lesson: The growth or the stagnation of myself. If the message reveals that I should not trust again or try again or love again or forgive, then I know that my view is not through the eyes of love, but fear! When I shift to seeing with love I always end up with a happy ending! In truth my stories are probably yours, just told in a different voice, and if all else fails, laugh!

Lillian Gish soon after she started acting in Hollywood.

Chapter 1

Lillian Gish
To Be Continued

Those who bring sunshine to others
Cannot keep it from themselves.

– James Barrie

The title of this chapter was born from another book about another life in another time. How, of all the titles in the world, I chose this one is more about how it chose me. During my television days in Dallas, many writers and actors criss-crossed the big cities promoting their books, or movies, or both. Their public relations people would scout out the talk shows on television and radio and decide where their client would best fit. A phone call would be made to the program producer and if the guest sounded interesting or had a significant name, a booking on the show would be offered. The bigger the fame of the guest, the more time would be allotted for airplay.

When the telephone call came to me offering the great actress, Miss Lillian Gish, I knew I would need at least thirty minutes with her. Remember, in the Seventies television was not about cramming a good fifteen minute interview into two shallow minutes, or a "sound bite." We had, back then, the time to give because we were not as interested in dedicating every precious minute to a commercial. We didn't run six or eight commercials in a row because we were dedicated to providing good and interesting programming. That was the challenge then. Look at what is offered today … see the difference?

She was coming, "Miss Lillian Gish". She was coming to our studio and she was going to sit at our old round oak interview table and I was going to get to ask her about her career, starting at the very first silent movie classic, *Birth of a Nation.* She had made a zillion films, she had traversed the silent screen era into the "talking picture" stage. She was magnificent at any role she undertook: as the ingénue in *Birth of a Nation,* to the crusty, determined grandmother in the chilling *Night of the Hunter.* She, to me, epitomized the perfect lady — generous, witty, well groomed, understated, and compassionate but nobody's fool. Generally, the only preparation I did for an interview was by reading a book about or by the guest, view the movie the celebrity was promoting, study the subject we were going to discuss, and then, just go with an opening statement and let the process of listening and responding take its course. I never had a list of questions. In real life, we don't have a list of questions. We say hello, and then see what happens next. Interviewing is less about asking questions and more about listening to what the guest says and keying in on that … it is called "conversation."

For Miss Lillian Gish, I would prepare. I mean there were so many things I wanted to know about her, the close sister of Dorothy who was her younger sibling. About the "unmarried" Miss Gish; the travels she had taken on film locations all over the world; the clothes which were created for her and the mother and father she left behind when she toured the world working with the great director, D.W. Griffith.

Dorothy and Lillian Gish were inseparable as sisters. They were bound less by blood, and more by friendship and an inexplicable connection. Their rollicking adventures as little girl leading ladies, and young women whose strength and radiance emanated from the black and white flickering moving pictures, took their audiences from innocence to life's pain and beyond survival to conquering victory. They were part of each other from birth till Dorothy's death.

They made films together, and separately each were admired and applauded for her own talent. Dorothy had a long and glorious marriage to an adoring husband and Lillian remained married to the movies and her career. She was like a second mother to her nieces and they were like her own children. She never despaired of being childless herself. It was about the time they spent together that was the purpose of her tour across the United States as not only a celebrated actress but as the author of her book entitled *The Gishes: Dorothy and Lillian.* I had not yet received a copy of the book so I could not include it in my preparation for the interview.

It was off to the library for me. Gathering a pile of books and rushing home excited to begin a weekend of research, I imagined there would be no time for sleep. Boy! Was I wrong. I stacked the twelve loaned books on my dining table, picked up the first one, which happened to be an autobiography entitled *D. W. Griffith and Me,* randomly opened it to the dedication and read:

"To my mother who taught me to love;
To my sister who taught me to laugh;
To my father who taught me the 'wisdom of insecurity;'
To D.W. Griffith who taught me 'it is more fun to work
Than to play.' "

That was it for me! After that what else did I need? Her four special sentences showed me the heart and soul of this diminutive, beautiful, lyrical woman. The focus of my first question would be "the wisdom of insecurity." In the 70s we were exploring ourselves more than at any other time in my lifetime. *Transcendental Meditation. I'm Okay, You're Okay, Born to Win, Why Am I Afraid to Tell You Who*

I Am. These books were all best sellers because we couldn't get enough of learning about why we were like we were; how we could grow deeper and feel more of everything. If we felt any insecurity we rushed to the neighborhood "shrink" to unravel the problems of not measuring up, which we blamed on our parents. I mean we blamed everything on our parents. Insecurity was the big one. I slept soundly that Sunday night, sure of where we would go in the interview Monday morning.

Her entrance to the studio was not grand; she came as a guest into a new home. She smiled, greeted everyone from the director to the camera crew. The lighting engineer was so excited to meet her that he personally arranged a floor level light just for her. I had wanted my own floor level light for two years. Studio light was ceiling height. When it lit you from above, your eye lashes cast a shadow that made you look like you had "bags under your eyes." It's the way they do in "Hollywood". Lighting you straight on. Oh! I wanted that light. I told Miss Gish how I had begged for one and she gently chided the "boys" for not giving me what I wanted. We all laughed knowing that I was no "Lillian Gish".

As we waited to go on the air, I happened to notice her beautiful brooch. She took a little gasp and touched my hand and thanked me for noticing it. Then she quietly told me that it belonged to Dorothy, her sister, and closest companion and best friend, who had died two years before. She said, "today is the first day since her death that I could bear to wear it … I miss her so. How wonderful that you would notice it and mention it. I feel as though she must be with me now. Thank you, my dear."

We settled into our chairs, silently waiting for the glow of the red camera light indicating that we were "on the air." We were like two excited thoroughbreds waiting for the clang of the bell and the starter gates to burst open on Derby Day. All was quiet and then the red light came on.

Unplanned, I took her hand and explained to the camera and the audience that watched from home, about my elation over being in the presence of "Miss Lillian Gish." I told of my resolve to be prepared and read everything about her so that I could use our time together to charm the television audience as she had charmed us in her motion pictures we watched, felt and never forgot. And then, I opened the auto-biography that she had written (I could tell by the squeeze on my hand that she was pleased). I read the dedication and then turned to her and said, "Miss Gish … The Wisdom of Insecurity? Most of us think of this as a flaw, something in us that needs fixing. What is the wisdom in it?"

Her twinkling blue eyes and gentle smile reinforced her resolve that "without insecurity we would never strive to overcome the difficult: without insecurity we would give in to complacency and never know what we are capable of achieving or what if need be, we can endure. Insecurity is not a flaw … it's a gift from God."

The studio was silent … all of us enrapt in her melodious voice and honest inspiration. We knew we were in the presence of a truly unique, decent and fine person. She was tinier in stature than we expected but she was a presence that all of us, long after the interview ended, felt grateful to have been part of that day.

We talked, she and I, of her passion for work; the joy of it. The gratitude for the experiences she had; the people the places; the hotels and tents she bunked in along the trail of her rise to stardom. No, she did not regret never marrying, although she had loved deeply … she did not go further. There was no need to. Then as she told of the love of her sister and mother and father; the gaiety of their adventures and the blessed sharing of their lives with each other, she opened her new book that lay on the table and began to discuss some of the pictures. I held it up so that the camera could show the audience and as I turned the last page in the book my heart literally stood still for an instant.

There was a faded full length photograph of two little girls about twelve years old or so, with their backs to the camera, standing side by side in little white pinafore dresses with ruffles on their shoulders and full white skirts tied at the waist with a big bow. They wore wide brim straw hats with black grosgrain ribbon tied around the crown. Their long ringlet curls cascaded down their backs. They stood close together, proudly straight and confident of the road that lay ahead of them. It was as if they were walking toward that road and we were seeing them off on their journey. They were the Gishes … Dorothy and Lillian … one gone on and the other ending an interview in Dallas Texas. Below the photograph in tiny lettering off to the right hand side … it simply read "to be continued." I have to tell you, I could barely speak to go to a commercial break.

I was so moved that if I had spoken it would have been quivery and maudlin. We just held the camera on the photograph and left it there as the credits rolled ending the show. The crew gave me some Kleenex and took some for themselves. Miss Gish and I stayed at the table and talked together, with the crew gathered round, for the next hour. It was the most memorable, precious, unexpected time. It was one of the those gifts. Telling about it makes it live again in my memory.

I told Miss Gish that if I ever wrote a book I was going to title a chapter *To Be Continued.* It is a perfect description of life. No, it is a perfect description of the "hope in life;" relationships which are put on hold, at some time down the road will be reconnected … to be continued. The hope of life after this one … to be continued … a career put on hold to raise a family … to be continued. A conversation with a warm and gentle movie star unpretentious in her opinion of herself and a promise by a star struck young woman starting over once again … to remember her always through this book … *If All Else Fails, Laugh!*

Loving wishes
from
The Gishes.
Lillian and Dorothy..

To be continued

Unknown, Clint Eastwood and Suzie (He might have been sitting on a barstool.)

Chapter 2

The Day Clint Eastwood Dropped By

If all else fails, Laugh!

– Suzie Humphreys

Back in 1970, the biggest movie star in the world was Clint Eastwood. He was the number one box office attraction all over the world. He didn't do interviews. He didn't like the press. He didn't trust the press and because he was so private and famous, didn't need the press. I was working in television hosting a morning show in Dallas with the ABC affiliate, WFAA. Clint Eastwood was coming to town to do some hunting with a buddy of his who was also in broadcasting, Gordon McClendon. Gordon was well known in Texas but had a string of famous associates in Hollywood and the likes, and he happened to be a master of promotion. He also owned a big theatre in Dallas which he had offered to Clint Eastwood, to roll out the world premiere of his *Dirty Harry* film. He asked me if I would be interested in doing an interview with Eastwood to help promote the film. Believe me, that was the biggest and most important question anyone had ever asked me and I jumped to it with a "Yes!"

I knew I didn't want to interview Clint Eastwood in an orange chair in a studio. No, I wanted to do something really different, like have him over to my place and cook dinner for him. Why not, I thought. I would set a cozy little table for two. There would be crystal and champagne. I would be cooking the sauce, and when the doorbell rang, I would sweep to the door, fling it open and there would be Clint Eastwood. My camera crew would capture it all on film and we would play the entire interview to coincide with the film's opening. I asked his manager if "Mr." Eastwood would agree and he said he would.

On the day of the interview, I got up as I always did at three-thirty in the morning and got ready to be on the air at seven o'clock. As I left my apartment, I backed out of my driveway and eased past the vacant lot that had been empty out my back door forever and I headed down to the studio. The world around me was dark, the vacant lot was empty and the day was no different than it had ever been. I was off to a good start!

I finished the Morning Show at nine, took care of business for the next day, and hurried home to get ready for the one o'clock. interview with Clint Eastwood. I pulled into the driveway and passed the vacant lot that was no longer vacant! There were nine yellow Caterpillars on it breaking ground for a shopping center. It sounded like a war zone! I knew we were in trouble. I knew we could not film with noise like this, so I just changed gears. I ran upstairs to telephone Clint Eastwood's manager and suggest another location. That was simple enough, except that everyone had already left. They were on their way. They had stopped off for lunch, and I had no idea where they were. I couldn't stop them! The clock was ticking.

I stood out on my balcony, looking out at those nine yellow Caterpillars, trying to think of something to do when, all of a sudden, I noticed that one of those Caterpillars had a little umbrella over the driver. I figured he must be the foreman. You certainly wouldn't think they'd give the umbrella to the "new" guy. I walked out across the ditches and trenches and pot holes of that vacant lot, wearing my three inch lizard shoes, and marched right up to the guy under the umbrella. I motioned to him and he killed the machine. I yelled at him, "Clint Eastwood is coming to my place."

He looked at me like I was out of my mind and hollered back, "We're just real thrilled about that lady."

"No," I said, "you don't understand. I'm going to do this interview with him, and you guy's are making too much noise."

"We're real sorry," he sputtered, wiping the dust and sweat and grime off his face.

"Look, this is not a problem, let's just coordinate coffee breaks," I suggested.

"What do you mean?" he questioned.

I gave my biggest smile, cocked my head to one side and said, "When we're ready to shoot film, you guys can take your break."

"We don't take breaks," he shouted.

"Get serious," I volleyed back. Then we started jawing back and forth and things got heated. I stormed off and he cranked up the Caterpillar, moving out and moving away from that nut that was fixing to cry.

I got back to my apartment and tried to think of something to save this fiasco. I was feeling like a fool when I heard a loud knock at my back door. I jerked it open and there stands the foreman.

"Lady," he said, "I've changed my mind. I'll do it for you."

I threw my arms around him and hugged him. I thanked him till it got boring. We planned our strategy, got our signals all straight between us and he goes back to the Caterpillars.

My camera man arrives and we set up the lights. My door bell rings. I sweep to the door. I open it and there stands Clint Eastwood. Now this may be an every day occurrence in some people's lives, but it was a big deal to me. And when you meet somebody famous, you don't want to be stupid! You don't want to stammer and spit out the same dumb thing most people would say like, "Hi. You look like you do in the movies."

Words just failed me. I wanted to say something different, something nobody else had ever said before, something really memorable. But when I opened my mouth the words just tumbled out. "Listen, you're the number one box office attraction all over the world but I'm real big in Dallas." He just stood there, frozen. Didn't move or blink. He didn't even change expressions. I reached for his hand (I actually held his hand) and said, "Come on. I'll show you."

I dragged him out on the balcony, and there were nine yellow Caterpillars churning up the ground below us. I flung out my arms and waved them like an umpire calling "Safe," and they stopped!

Clint got a little smile in the corner of his mouth and said, "That's real good." Then he kicked my shoe with his boot and whispered. "Are you going to tell me the story behind this?"

I drawled, "Nothing, I'm just big in parking lots and vacant lots." We went back inside and started the interview. During the conversation, every now and then he'd squeeze my hand and say, "I don't want to talk about my movie, I just want to know the story behind those Caterpillars."

When we finished the interview I took him back on the balcony, and there were nine yellow Caterpillars sitting there silent as stones. I threw up my arms, snapped my fingers again, and, on cue, the engines roared to a start and off they rolled.

Two weeks later, I got a letter from Clint Eastwood thanking me for the time in Dallas, and down at the bottom he wrote, "I'm still talking about the girl in Dallas and those yellow Caterpillars. I can't wait to see what you've got for me next time!"

Next time! I did two more interviews in the next two years with the man who didn't do interviews. His manager would call, out of the blue, and say, "Sooz, Clint's coming to town and wants to know if you want to do anything."

I answered, "Sure, but you can't put it on TV!"

This story seems unbelievable, but you know even in the oddest situations there is a point. Do you know why I was able to get those two more interviews? It was because of those nine yellow Caterpillars … the worst thing I thought that could possibly happen to me that day. If it hadn't been for those Caterpillars, we would have had just an ordinary old interview. He would have flown out of town that day and never even remembered my name. But the Caterpillars made something spontaneous and fun and off the wall happen. If it's fun, we always want to do it again. Clint did. Those nine yellow Caterpillars made our day!

So look for the unexpected to rearrange life in the most unexpected ways. The universe always seems to have a better plan in mind … even one that, at first glance, feels like a disaster.

Rachel Malone, Suzie's mother

Chapter 3

My Mom and Me

Perhaps I ain't relijus, But when I say a prayer, I sort of feel inside of me that God and Mom is always there.

— John Mant

My mom left my dad in the dead of night. After fourteen years of marriage, she decided to make it on her own. That was in the early Forties, and even though the norm for women then was to be a homemaker, my mom had a job. She worked at Firestone Tire and Rubber Company and her job description was to do anything that needed doing. That ranged from pumping gasoline, bookkeeping, selling Philco radios, and making the customers smile. She did all of those duties well, especially the smiling part. The customers loved her. She always laughed while she worked and pepped everyone up, even with the war going on. She was pretty too. She was small, with curly brown hair and rich brown eyes. She had that hourglass figure and great legs which were mostly covered up by the white coveralls she wore that read Rachel on the breast pocket. She had been happy at her job, but now with me to raise alone, two problems presented themselves: Where were we going to live, and what was she going to do with me during the day?

What Mom wanted, what she began to visualize, was a beautiful home in a nice part of San Antonio, owned by an elderly lady who lived alone, who would be willing to rent a room to a working mother and look after a child in the daytime. Within four days Mom found her. Her name was Mamaduke Phillips. She lived in a large, beautiful two-story English Tudor home, and she was used to having children around. She had four of her own, though they were all grown. Mamaduke opened her home to us and we became her new family: three generations of women. Because I was only four years old, I remember only little glimpses of that time, but my best memory of Mamaduke's was when my mom came home at the end of the day. My mother was everything to me, and the house just seemed to sing when she walked in the door; the sound of her laughter and the click of her shoes against the hardwood floor, the way her voice went up and down the scale when she talked, the words she spoke, the way she smelled, the way she cooked — I adored all of these things about this bigger-than-life tiny woman.

Among her many customers at Firestone was Mr. S. E. McCreeless, the owner of American Hospital and Life Insurance Co. Recognizing that Mother was so great with the customers, Mr. S. E. mentioned to her that if she ever decided to leave Firestone, he would have a place for her in the insurance industry.

She responded with, "Do you think I could make a lot of money?"

He said, "I do!"

Two weeks later she quit her full-time salaried job at Firestone and appeared at Mr. S. E.'s office carrying a brand-new briefcase. She said, "I'm ready to go to work!"

My mother was placed with sixteen men and one other woman in the agency. The agents sold the insurance plans, and even though she didn't know anything about insurance, she was a fast learner. In fact she was one of the top five producers that year. A bear hunt was their reward. The male dominated insurance industry chose to honor its best sales people with recognition that only men might appreciate. But Mom went on the bear hunt to Montana. She literally hit the ground running selling insurance. She loved selling insurance. She believed she was being of service to people, and she liked feeling that she was helping. Group insurance had not been initiated, so you sold to an individual who was head of the household (that usually meant male), and you called on him early in the morning before he went to work or at the end of his business day — at home and after dinner. This meant that my mother was usually gone by six in the morning and not home until after eight, and sometimes ten o'clock. But on the weekends she was mine; she would take me with her every-where, even when she made calls out of town.

My mom never drove on the highway under eighty-five miles per hour in her life. We would begin each trip with Mom sliding behind the wheel of the car, turning to me with a big smile on her face and saying, "I love to drive." We would strike off! We'd have hard-boiled eggs, triple-decker tuna fish sandwiches and Cokes in the little green glass bottles packed in the ice chest. We'd get about four blocks from home, start eating those sandwiches and we'd just laugh. And, oh, we would sing! Mom taught me to harmonize when I was five; she would sing melody and I'd sing harmony to "Carolina in the Morning." She always carried a loaded shotgun in the back seat floorboard. This was not for protection, you understand, it was because she was a Texas woman and when you traveled those dusty South Texas roads, you were certain to find a lot of doves sitting on the phone wires. When she'd see them ahead, she would slowly stop the car, quietly open the door, get her shotgun, and Bam! Bam! Two or three doves would fall. She would then turn to me and order, "Go get 'em, Suzanne." Because my job was to watch where they dropped, I knew exactly where to fetch them. We'd laugh and start talking about how she was going to cook those doves that night. Of course, we had to get about eight or ten more in order to have a really good mess of them.

We were traveling to Houston one Friday, cruising at about ninety miles per hour and singing "Sonny Boy," when Mom looked in the rearview mirror and said, "Uh-oh."

I said, "What's wrong, Mom?"

She replied, "Cop in the rearview mirror." I will never forget those comforting words as she leaned across the seat to me and said, "Hold On!" Her foot slammed down on the accelerator, she sped off the interstate down a country road, ducked behind some poor farmer's barn, and watched that patrolman speed down the road leaving a cloud of dust in his trail. She had outsmarted the patrolman! That was my mom!

When I was starting to school, Mom came home one day and said, "Suzie, we are getting ourselves an apartment." An apartment! This meant our own place with our own kitchen and one bedroom. We didn't have much furniture, but she bought two twin beds and a dresser for the bedroom. For the empty living room she bought a piano! She figured the sofa and chairs would come later. The piano was her most treasured possession! She never took a music lesson in her life, but she could sit down and play any song after hearing the melody one time.

I spent a lot of time by myself. People in the apartment would keep an eye out for me, but I really watched out for myself. I never got bored because I had my radio and I loved all the old programs. I also liked to draw and cut out pictures from magazines. I could cook and get myself to school, I made friends easily and I sang a lot too. The school was always having me sing for functions, but for some reason I was reluctant to tell my mom or my dad when he picked me up from school. Life from my perspective was very normal. I knew, of course, that other kids didn't live like I did, but I never spent much time thinking about that.

My mom came home one day and said, "Suzie, we are getting a two-bedroom apartment." Wow! My own room. After two more years it was, "Suzie, we are renting a house." Mom was moving up in the insurance world. She was driving a Cadillac, she had more shoes than Imelda Marcos, she had over 100 bottles of perfume on a small mirrored vanity, and if she found a suit she liked, she'd buy it in every color they made. The next logical step was, "Suzie, we are buying a house!"

For those wonderful early and adolescent years, my mother was my very purpose for existing. Then I hit *fourteen*. Something was to change between us, something that we could never get back. We could not spend five minutes in the same room without one of us getting angry or having our feelings hurt. My mother's life was stressed; her relationships kept her on an emotional roller coaster. She was tightening the reins on me, and I was used to being independent, fending for myself, making my own decisions, taking care of my own business. I rebelled, and she pulled in tighter. I dreaded the sound of her car pulling in the garage. I never looked forward to her coming home any more. It pained me, but I didn't know how to get back the feeling that I once had for her and I suspect that she felt the same way about me. This continued for *forty-four years!* We'd try to get our old relationship back, at Christmas or on the telephone, hoping the other would give what it was we thought we wanted. We always looked to the other to make up for the love that was missing in our lives. Because we were so close, we took out our frustrations on each other. I would shut her out of my life as a teenager, and she would release her anger at her job, or at "him," on me. I resented it, and all I wanted to do was to get away. I then began to compare my life to my friends', the ones who ate dinner as a family every night, who went to church and on vacations together, who had structure and balance and who seemed to be loved and comforted by their parents.

Looking back, my mom has been through the Cadillacs, the lake houses, the homes and the clothes. She has glaucoma and osteoporosis, but she is not totally debilitated. She has not been out of the house in almost three years because she likes to be familiar with her surroundings and feel in control. As long as she has *The Enquirer* once a week and *Judge Judy* every day, she is the most well-adjusted person I know. I have never heard her say, "If only," or "If only I hadn't."

Now my mom and I get along great, and she hasn't changed a bit! I have! I changed the way I looked at her. After forty-four years I started looking at what she *had* done for me, rather than what she *had not* done. I realized the priceless gifts she had given me:

- A sense of humor — the ability to laugh at myself and my mistakes.
- A sense of confidence — the ability to believe in myself and know that I am capable of anything.
- A sense of optimism — the ability to find the hope and the bright side in every situation.
- A sense of independence — the ability to take responsibility for my life and realize it is up to me to make it interesting or successful.

All of these things came from my mom. I saw her love to drive and to work. Consequently, I love to drive and to work! I saw her laugh and try everything that came her way. I have always tried to be on the stage, not in the audience watching, to go with whatever came along in my adventure of living, not be afraid to try, be willing to go with change, blow with the winds of life rather than to stay anchored by the chains of boredom and sameness. These are the real gifts given me by my mother.

Before I could see all of these as gifts, I had to first give up my resentments and "poor little Suzie" whining, and get down to the gut level business of forgiving her for not being what I thought she ought to be. One of the best ways I found to do this was by doing some small interview segments with her about her own childhood. To find out about her, I had to first find out about what it was like to live with her parents. Were they loving and outgoing, or were they fearful and undemonstrative toward their children?

What I found was not pleasant. Her father, an alcoholic who was abusive to her mother, died in my mother's arms when she was nine. She had feared and hated him, and as she held him in her arms beneath the hot afternoon sun on the dusty country road outside the family farm, she felt no sadness, only relief that perhaps their lives would be easier now that he was gone. My mother must have felt guilt about her feelings toward him. When we are angry or unloving toward anyone, regardless of what we perceive they have done to us, we don't like ourselves. From that point, as long as we carry those feelings, we not only resent that person, but we resent ourselves.

How would you tell a nine-year-old that her own healing would begin with forgiveness? For that matter, how do you tell a twenty-three- or a forty-year old? Forgiveness was not talked about years ago. Why? Didn't the *Bible* say an eye for an eye? Only saints forgave, we thought, and certainly no one we knew even remotely resembled a saint. And certainly if we were forgiving, it had to be given to another person; nobody taught us about forgiving ourselves.

At nine nears old, Mother began to carry a very large burden. As her life took her away from her mother and beloved grandparents, to live with a strict aunt and loving uncle, she carried additional anger with her. She kept it hidden deep inside so no one would see. She did not know how to rationalize that it was because of money that she had been sent away. The family's breadwinner was now dead, and two of the other five children had to live with relatives. Two years later, Mom's mother and grandparents both died within six months, and Mother was sent home on a train to attend their funerals.

I, as Mother's daughter, now saw her in a much different light. So many things about her were now obvious to me. So many "nothing" slights by her in my life now became totally irrelevant compared to what she had endured. Where there was resentment, there was now compassion. Talk about making lemonade out of lemons — let's hear it for my mother.

Dr. Gerald Jampolsky, in his book entitled *Forgiveness: The Greatest Healer of All,* writes that forgiving others is the first step to forgiving ourselves.

Now it was up to *me* to forgive her for all the things I thought she had or had not done to me. Now it was up to *me* to forgive myself for being young and carrying all of that young anger with me through my relationships and life. Now it was up to *me* to use the lessons from my mother for my son Josh, to learn from her not only how to be but how *not* to be with a child.

I am grateful to her always for her example. I am grateful to God that I have finally been able to change my perception of her, for it is in changing perception that one is able to realize the greatest joys of our past. It is only when we look at another in a different perspective that we are able to forgive them for not measuring up to our own expectations. It is only in changing our perspective of the past that we are able to see the present in the brightest and holiest light.

My Aunt Suzie, my mom, Rachel E. Malone, seated, and me.

News 8 — 1972 — The great clown Emitt Kelly, Suzie, Don Harris my co-host and producer We three "clowns" performed with Ringling Brothers Circus.

Chapter 4

She's My First Customer

Success is when the unexpected happens.
— Harry Smith

I had been encouraging my friend Sally Ross to do some speaking. Certainly she had the most wonderfully funny and fascinating stories to tell because the things that have happened to her are proof that truth is stranger than fiction. We were brainstorming over coffee one day; I was fired up about the possibilities of her standing before a group of people and blindsiding them with her wit and inimitable way of speaking. I said, "The only thing you have to figure out, Sally, is what's the point of the stories. You see, before you open your mouth you've got to know where you want to end up! The point."

My partner, Ron Chapman, passed on that rule to me early in my radio career. It was the rule each on-air person had to live by so that we would not be rambling on and on, never knowing when to shut up! Sally looked perplexed and said, "I don't know what the point is."

"Tell me the story then, and let's see if we can figure it out," I said.

This is what she related: "It was in the early '70s and I had just received my license to sell real estate. I had an understanding, but busy, husband, and two kids in diapers at home. The company I went to work for put me on Sunday phone duty. That meant if the phone rang I answered it and tried to help the person on the other end of the line. It was winter, cold and rainy, and nothing had gone on in the office since I went on duty at noon. It was now five-forty and I had only twenty minutes left until I could go home and feed the family. All at once, the phone rang. It actually rang.

"I thought it was my husband telling me to hurry up and get home 'cause they were starving. I answered, 'Hello,' and an unfamiliar voice said, 'I saw an ad in the Sunday paper today for a house that was listed for $19,000.' I perked up. 'Yes, ma'am, we have that house. May I ask your name?' 'Klein,' she responded, 'Wilva Klein.' I quickly followed with, 'What time tomorrow would you like to see the house?' She said, 'Now!'

"'Now?' I stammered. 'Now,' she emphasized. 'How long will it take you to pick me up? I'm at a 7 Eleven at the intersection of Seventh and Fitzhugh.'

"I spit out, 'Thirty minutes.' After all, she was my first customer, and I didn't care what it took, I wasn't going to let her get away.

"I hung up the phone, called home, and listened to my husband rant on. I did feel guilty about the kids crying, but with the commission I'd make on a $19,000 house, I'd take them to Kiddie Land for unlimited rides.

"I threw diapers, empty Coke bottles and Snickers wrappers into the trunk of my ten-year-old Cutlass, and off I went to pick up my 'first customer.' She was standing in the mist under a street lamp, and she was a lot smaller than her booming voice revealed. I rolled down the window and introduced myself, and she got in the back seat! I said, 'Mrs. Klein, wouldn't you rather ride up front?' She clipped, 'This will do,' So off we went!

"I tried to make polite, get-to-know-you conversation, but she only responded with one word replies — yes or no! Finally I asked her, 'How many are in your family?' She answered, 'I have six children and a husband.' 'Hmm,' I mused, 'how are eight people going to live in a $19,000 house? Wouldn't you like to see something bigger?' 'No, she snapped. 'The house I called about is the one I wish to see.'

"'Good,' I said. I lied.

"The house was small, empty and dark when we arrived. As I guided her through the tour, I noticed that her little wispy birdlike hands held a tiny spiral notebook upon which she wrote furiously. I kept leaning over to see what she was writing, but I couldn't get a clear view. She made no comment about the house, not good, bad, or otherwise, and as I guided her out the front door, she said, 'What do you have to show me tomorrow?' I rallied. 'Tomorrow, Mrs. Klein, I'll have a good selection to show you. What time should I pick you up and where?' A tinge of suspicion crept over me when she replied, 'nine in the morning at the same 7 Eleven.' I drove home, dreading to hear my husband gripe, but excited that I actually had a *customer* … my first customer.

"The next day at the Monday morning meeting, I jubilantly told of my night adventure with Mrs. Klein. It was the general consensus that I had a dud! In time, they echoed, I'd learn to spot those people who were wasting my time.

"'But she's my first customer,' I said.

"On to Wilva at the 7 Eleven. She was waiting impatiently; I could tell by the way her arms were crossed and she was tapping her foot, but luckily I had organized our day according to available houses in her price range. Over the next seven hours we looked at ten houses. At no time did she ever indicate any interest or disinterest in the properties. She just kept scribbling in that little spiral notebook. We rode in silence except for when she wanted me to pull into another 7 Eleven for lunch. I waited in the car while she bought food for herself. She never offered me a bite, but what the heck ... *she was my first customer!* When I dropped her off in the late afternoon, she said, 'I'll expect you at nine sharp tomorrow morning.'

"By now I was the laughingstock of the office. Maybe I was, I thought, but this lady needs a house and I'm going to help her find it! Day two was just like day one; no sale, no comment, no lunch ... just be there the next morning at nine. By this time we had looked at more than twenty houses! It was hard for me to keep my spirits up.

"Day three began much like the others. I told Mrs. Klein that we had only seven houses left to see. She indicated that would be fine, as she had to be at the airport by mid-afternoon. Mid-afternoon? That didn't leave me much time.

"My first customer was leaving on a jet plane at three o'clock. I was going to spend the next years of my career banished to phone duty because I had wasted my time on a woman who was (to quote my co-workers) not a serious buyer. Oh, well, I thought, it's not over till it's over. I've still got five hours and *she was my first customer.*

"As we walked through the last house and she scribbled her final notes in the little spiral notebook, I smiled cheerfully (what a fake!) and meekly asked, 'Mrs. Klein, of the twenty-seven houses, which one do you like?' Opening the little book, she quickly flipped the pages and said, 'I'll take number 2, 4, 6, 7, 13, 14, 16,' and so on. *Wilva Klein bought seventeen houses that day. My first customer bought seventeen houses.*"

When Sally finished the story, I fell on the floor laughing. "Gosh, Sally," I said, "What a story." She was laughing too, but through the squeals she said, "You should have seen the faces on the people at the office, especially when I was named rookie of the year my first year in the business!"

Then quickly she asked, "Suzie, what do you think is the point?"

"It's obvious," I replied. "The point is to treat everyone like she is your first customer, no matter how small the possibility of the sale. The importance should be placed on the client, not on the people who try to discourage you. If we focus on being of service and helping and that's all, before we know it, that bell on the cash register will be ringing in a steady rhythm."

Earlier that year, I was reading Kirk Douglas's fascinating biography, *Climbing the Mountain ... My Search for Meaning.* In the very beginning of the book he quoted Viktor Frankl, the author of *Man's Search for Meaning.* "This remarkable book," he said, "will be etched in the memory of every reader who has the privilege to discover it." It was named one of the ten most influential books in America in the 1991 Library of Congress/Book-of-the-Month Club Survey of Lifetime Readers. This is the passage that Mr. Douglas quoted:

> *"Don't aim at success — the more you aim at it and make it a target, the more you are going to miss it. For success, like happiness, cannot be pursued; it must ensue, and it only does so as the unintended side-effect of one's dedication to a cause greater than oneself or as the by-product of one's surrender to a person other than oneself. Happiness must happen, and the same holds for success: you have to let it happen by not caring about it. I want you to listen to what your conscience commands you to do and go on to carry it out to the best of your knowledge. Then you will live to see that in the long run — in the long run, I say — success will follow you precisely because you had forgotten to think of it!"*

Andy Devine, the lovable actor with the squeaky voice.

Chapter 5

This Too Shall Pass

Win the world by doing the unexpected.
— Thomas Hardy

As I mentioned earlier, the movies were my baby sitter! The Forties movies — the days of black and white, of cigarettes smoked in long holders, of big shoulder pads and waspish waists. I would sit in the front row with a giant box of popcorn and look up to those wonderful heroes and villains. In the Westerns, there was always a sidekick, the jovial bumblesome pal who was never far from the side of the hero. Though he was never as handsome or agile, never as horse-capable (he always rode on the chuckwagon), he was forever loyal, and come what may, he always smiled.

One such character stepped right out of the screen and into my life in the Seventies. His name was Andy Devine, and I remembered him vividly as Jingles, Roy Rogers' sidekick. The long gray sideburns that curled just around his ears made him look like a kindhearted sea captain, but his drawl and laugh and portly belly could not disguise that he was still a cowboy through and through.

He and his lovely wife arrived at the TV station several minutes early, and while the crew was getting the set ready, the three of us chatted at the coffee bar. I was struck by his presence. He seemed genuinely cheerful and uplifting. He was warm and appreciative that we had invited him to be on the show. He was interested in my life and how long I'd worked in television. He wanted to know about the new baby one of the crew members and his wife had recently brought home from the hospital. Although we didn't talk about anything specific, it was fun just to be in his presence. Because he and his wife held hands the whole time, I asked how long they had been married. I was not surprised when he responded with, "Forty years." They fit well together. I wasn't sure what we were going to talk about, and memory fails me now as to why he was on a promotional tour, but I knew that whatever he said, people would enjoy hearing him.

We settled into our two orange interview chairs. The set lights came on. The floor chief gave us a countdown to broadcast time. Looking at the camera, I said to the audience, "In the movies he was Roy Rogers' best friend. You and I knew him then as Jingles. Today I'm happy to introduce you to Mr. Andy Devine." Then turning to him I added, "If the truth were known, you are probably still Roy's best friend."

He laughed a slow rolling kind of laugh that begins in a bass tone and rises to falsetto. He said, "I hope so. I treasure all my friendships."

"Friends must come easily to you because you appear to be so happy. Am I right about that? Have you always been happy?" I asked.

"Oh, pretty much I guess. Except that one bad time."

I sat up quickly and followed with, "What time was that?" This is the story he told:

"I was nineteen, and movies were just coming into their own. I knew I wanted to be an actor. I wanted to ride horses and chase the bad guys. You didn't have to have any credentials, just know how to ride (which I did) and how to fire a blank from a six-shooter.

"I saved the whopping sum of $300 and left my home, bound for Hollywood. I rented a garage apartment in a modest residential neighborhood close to a bus line, got myself an agent, had some publicity pictures made, and called myself an 'actor'. The daily routine was to get to the studios early, stand in line and try to get a part in the day's filming as an extra. By the end of the first week I was well known to the studios but had not been cast in any of their pictures. I told myself then that no one makes it the first week, but in the second week I'd have a job! I scrimped on spending and really, the only expense I had outside of bus fare and apartment rent was food. I have always been a big man, so I required a lot of sustenance. Even then, I tried to save money by eating sandwiches and soup and crackers. Nothing fancy.

"Week two rolled into week three. My agent sent me on a couple of auditions, and always I'd go in with high hopes and come out with rejection. My money was dwindling and so was my confidence! Depression began to creep into my jovial nature, and by the end of the third week I was so down I decided that if I didn't get a job in the movies before my money ran out, I didn't want to live anymore. Life simply held no meaning for me. If I couldn't act, I did not want to live. There it was! No acting, no life. I would kill myself!

"By the time seven weeks had passed, things were very desperate. I only had twenty-five bucks left. Soon I started skipping meals but never the rounds of the studios. I was so down on myself that I was convinced if I did not get work, it wasn't meant for me to live. It was a sign.

"The money was gone in no time. One last time I made the rounds; one last time, nothing happened. I hadn't eaten for two days and when I got off the bus at sundown and walked past the neighborhood shops and cafes, I saw people with their families eating juicy hamburgers and fries. I watched them laugh and order another slice of pie. I was hungry, tired and hurt. Tonight, I concluded, when I got home I would do it! I would kill myself. I'd simply turn on the gas in my apartment, close all the windows, and be gone. It would be painless and over.!

"As night fell, I rounded the corner to my street and approached my little apartment where one small light bulb glowed over the entry door. As I reached out to put the key in the lock, determined to end my life, I saw a slip of paper hanging on the doorknob. Holding it in the light I read, 'Due to nonpayment of your bill, your gas has been turned off!' Written in ink below the notice was the word, 'Over.' On the backside scrawled in a semi-legible handwriting was a message from my agent. It said, 'Good news! Republic Studios called today and you've got the part.'"

There was an audible gasp that exploded into laughter from the visitors and floor crew in the studio, and after I had regained my composure, I asked, "Andy, what do you think the story has been telling you all these years?"

He chuckled and replied, "Well, whenever things don't always go my way, I guess you could say I always wait for them to change the way they're supposed to. I remember the unpaid gas bill, the way I felt so desolate and alone, the way a lot of people do at times throughout their lives. Then I think, what if the gas had not been turned off? I would have missed the whole big play, the wonderful life I've had all these years. I would have missed my kids, my wife, laughing, traveling, sharing, food, friends, and seeing the sunrise. I wouldn't have known the joy of fishing in a good stream on a fall day or finishing a movie that I was proud to be part of. I would have missed it all just because I had run out of hope. The point the story taught me was that things always get better. Like the *Bible* says, 'This too shall pass.' It has carried me all through my life and I haven't been down since!"

I have carried Andy Devine with me all these years. He gave all of us a little miracle that day, and even though he has been dead for many years, as I recount his words now, I believe he's still giving us that special feeling.

Richard Harris and Suzie

Chapter 6

Richard Harris

The perfect woman is a dead sinner, revised, edited and reissued.

– Richard Harris

His reputation as a "renegade" proceeded him. He was a "drinker," and was sometimes subject to a bar fight or two. He was a ladies man but a man's man too. He was a prankster, a poet, a proud Irishman, and a problem if challenged to defend his political views. He was the actor Richard Harris and for one half of a day I got to spend some time with him — a fun, enlightening, exciting time. The photographs prove it.

The music of the Seventies still carries me back to dance floors where high heeled women and booted men glided in a sensual rhythm to songs that made you feel Alive! Really Alive. From the moment you stepped on the dance floor, you *were* John Travolta … You *were* His partner. You were fabulous and you were free! I still love the Bee Gees and can relive every disco step to *Saturday Night Fever.* Donna Summer, and Gladyce Knight and the Pips … just take me to that dance floor once more for one final twirl. We were dancers, we were "movin" … we were "somebody"!

No song takes me back to the Seventies and ignites my fire like *MacArthur Park* and Richard Harris. I didn't just fall in love with the man ... I fell in love with his voice. I must have played that "record" ten times a day. I imagined that it was I who "left the cake out in the rain ... and that I could never have that recipe again ... Oh no!" John Travolta may have gotten us all on our feet once again, but it was Richard Harris who sang our "pain" and "sadness." I still get breathless just listening to him in my memory ... his smoky, husky, pained plea for love. I melted in MacArthur Park, I was made whole again in "Didn't We."

Well, big news for this television host in Dallas was that Richard Harris was coming to The Fairmont Hotel to perform his first ever night club act. And (trumpet blast) he would be doing MacArthur Park — the entire seven and one half minute version. Was this the best news I'd ever heard? Would I not only have a ring side table, I was going to interview him the next morning live at the television station. He was going to come in several days in advance of opening night and then we'd get the interview on the air the next day to bring in his fans.

I called Betty Holloway, the Fairmont Hotel's great and gracious PR director and booked the interview and claimed my seat for opening night ... which was always Press Night. I bought a fabulous new dress and the most amazing red lizard skin shoes (these were incidentally real lizard skin) and I could barely contain myself till the debut some weeks later. Every day after that I played MacArthur Park.

I learned that the week Harris arrived in Dallas there was a rumor abroad that my good friend and colleague Judy Jordan, the first news anchor woman in Dallas was to interview Harris while he lounged in bed, greeting her graciously, probably to shock her a bit. At least my interview with the actor would be more controlled, as it was to take place live at the television station the morning after his opening night! I couldn't wait for that night to come and the face to face meeting and interview next day.

The Venetian room at the Fairmont Hotel was filled with special guests and every member of the press corp. Dinner was fabulous, conversation was uplifting and witty and those of us who were lucky enough to be invited, clinked our wine goblets in a toast to each other and the pageantry of this extraordinary event which was highlighted by Richard's live musical performance. We wondered if his running buddies, Richard Burton and Peter O'Toole would be there to cheer him on. It was to us a "very big deal."

The stage was packed with the finest musicians, the lighting and sound checks had been completed, and then the house lights dimmed. The audience hushed, the conductor lifted his baton and, at his command, off stage came the musical preview: ta ta ta ta tatatatata. The announcer took the microphone and in an excited voice announced, "And now ladies and gentlemen the Fairmont Hotel is proud to present … Mr. Richard Harris." On cue, out Harris strolls on stage, confidently motioning a welcome to the audience. He lifts the microphone to his mouth … to those lips … croons, two words and then … stares at the audience silently … his eyes darting back and forth in a frightened plea … sweat beading on his forehead, the orchestra racing ahead of his place in the melody, leaving him to stand there lost and speechless until he finally wails, "Oh My God! I've forgotten the words."

The audience, with frozen doe-eyes and half hearted smiles, watched him collapse to the floor as he stared at the pink and blue stage lights overhead. Then, he shouted again as he kicked his feet, "Oh My God! I've really forgotten the words."

Then like a gymnast he sprang to his feet laughing, and shouted, "Let's try this thing again, shall we?"

"Yes," we cheered, applauding loudly as our energy boosted him up and gave him our full acceptance. We loved him!

We mouthed the words to all his songs, mothered him through MacArthur Park and wept for love lost. We gave him a standing ovation for five, no ten minutes at least … and it was over, ended, the evening, the amazing evening was over.

The next morning I arrived at the television station and while I was finishing my makeup our floor director Bob Cardenas asked, "Suzie what kind of set do you want for the Richard Harris interview? Two chairs, a sofa, what?"

I responded quickly, "No chairs, just a foot high stage or riser with carpet on it."

"Huh?" he quizzed.

"Yep! Just carpet. I'm gonna do the entire interview on the floor. He's most at home and at ease there."

As you can see, I was not only entertained the night before by Richard Harris, but I also learned a great lesson about the importance of making a guest feel comfortable. If I am comfortable with someone, I am more apt to be relaxed and open. That's when a good conversation can bring revelation and insight.

He was delighted — this Irishman with the gleam in his eye and the mischief in his heart. He saw the carpeted floor and cried "Where are the bloody chairs?"

Hoping my instincts were correct, I chuckled, "No chairs … we're just gonna sit on the floor."

He laughed and said, "Good lass … you saw the show last night?"

"Absolutely wonderful," I raved, "and my favorite seat in the house is the floor too."

"Good then," he teased, "I'll just stretch out and make myself at home!" With that he lay his head on my crossed leg and folded his hands across his belly, extended his legs, and we began this crazy but fun, quirky but interesting interview. We did sit up properly of course, after the joke to our TV audience had been played out, and conducted ourselves in a semi-professional manner ... although not too much so. We laughed and cajoled and poked fun and though today, some thirty-four years later, I cannot recall a single word of what we talked about it is the feeling of that interview with the warm and passionate Richard Harris that still glows in my mind. He was, for a time, a best friend, a brother and even the "star" that I had long had a crush on.

He hung around the studio with all of us and it was then that he revealed his patriotism and love of Ireland. He told us he had written a poem and if we would like, he would recite it and we could tape it to air on our Christmas show. We were overjoyed, to say the least. It was a long romantic poem filled with pain and pride about the conflict between the English and the Irish ... the Protestants and the

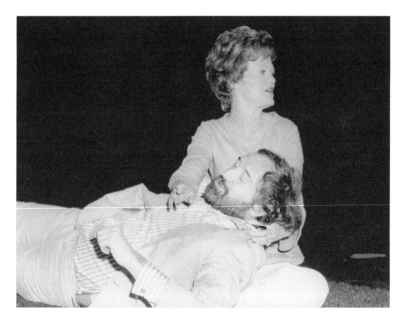

Suzie and Richard Harris

Catholics. The upheaval and the loss of lives caught in the crossfire had affected him to take action and use his status in the public eye to get all of us to care.

I don't remember the first time I pinched myself and whispered to myself and to God, "How did I get here?" I do know that I have been doing it for most of my life. "How did I get here" ... to sit and talk to Richard Harris, to have cocktails with Muhammed Ali and his beautiful wife, to shoot rifles with John Wayne, and ride a running horse in a buffalo roundup? How did I get to marry my amazing husband and have a glorious stepfamily and have a son whom I adore ... and own land in the country ... and get to travel the United States telling my stories? "Lord, why me?"

I think about it all the time and I suppose it's not important that I understand. What is important is the gratitude I feel for my time here. Appropriately, I recite to myself a poem called *Thank You Lord* written by the French monk Michael Quoist. It's about seeing gratitude in all of life, the small to the great. When I have a grateful heart I know that everything is a gift.

The poem can be found on page 156 of this book.

Suzie and Richard

Sammy Davis, Jr.

Chapter 7

Sammy Davis, Jr.

Dance in a rage of gusto;
Sing loud enough for the Lord to hear!

– Alvin Hart

I have often been asked "Out of all the interviews with famous people you've met, which was your favorite?" I don't have to think twice. It was and is Sammy Davis, Jr.

If you had asked me back then in the early Seventies who I thought was the most talented performer, I wouldn't have hesitated to repeat Sammy Davis, Jr's name. He could out dance anyone, play the horn like velvet, sing the ballad he made popular, *What Kind of Fool Am I?* and make your heart feel that you had been jilted by the greatest love of your life and still feel the loss long after the affair had ended. He could mimic all the famous people and he could keep up with them on stage. Just look how he fit in with Sinatra and the rest of the "Rat Pack."

Take the question a step further and ask me who I admired the least of the stars of that time, and I would reply … Sammy Davis, Jr. After all, he had publicly broken the unspoken code. A black man had married a white woman. The early Seventies was not ready for that. Not only were the "whites" not ready, the "blacks" weren't either. The highly publicized romance between Sammy and the beautiful German actress Mae Britt had caused tongues to wag throughout the country. Interracial marriages certainly took place ... but never were condoned publicly especially between two prominent celebrities. It was as though they were flaunting the taboo. Americans didn't like it because we were scared to death it might open the door for our kids to think it was acceptable. Then what? we wondered. Their children would be ostracized. We would have to leave our friends and home-places in disgrace.

I wish I could say I was different. I wish I could say interracial marriages didn't bother me. The truth is ... back then, I was like everyone else, scared to death that the beliefs I could stand firmly upon were being eroded. If this was alright what was the next to go?

I remember a variety television show in the late Sixties sponsored by Chrysler in which Petula Clark, the British pop singer whose hit recording of *Downtown* climbed to number one on the Billboard's top recordings, and Harry Belafonte, the handsome Jamaican singer and actor, hosted the hour-long special. All went well on the show, as both performers dazzled America with their fabulous voices and good looks. That is until the very end of the show, when the two strolled down the runway "arm in arm." There it was — a black man touching a white woman on national television. You could literally hear America gasping!

I had not been raised by Mother to be prejudiced. My father was, however. Strangely though, when he would make a remark about race or color, I would criticize him for it. It just didn't seem right to put anyone down or say that they "didn't know their place." I didn't like color barriers or implications that someone was better than anyone else. That included low lives, white trash, ignorants and those horrible names that we call someone so that we can make ourselves appear superior. My mother hired a wonderful woman when she and my father were still married. Her name was Ethel and she was a beautiful black woman who laughed all the time and hugged and loved me even more. She went everywhere with us. Everywhere, that is, which would allow her to enter. In many public places people of color had to "wait outside." It is horrible to think about that today. Back then, being young, not having yet learned hatred, I just knew I loved "my Ethie." Thanks to my mother, she did too.

Race was not an issue during my school years. As far as I can remember, poverty wasn't either. The "less fortunates" as polite society referred to the poor, just blended in with the "privileged." My wonderful friends in grade school through high school never showed any prejudice toward anyone. We just accepted everyone, except maybe the "loose" girls.

So how did I become one of the Americans gasping about racial blending? Fear, of course. Isn't that what's at the root of all hatred? Fear someone else will take what's mine, or get my place in line, or take away my values and force theirs upon me or you? I think today about this problem of fear, how it paralyzes us and keeps us from the greatest thing that brings us joy and peace ... and love. When we're doing what makes us happy and not worried about anything, or anybody we are truly free. Amazing: it isn't getting it that makes us the happiest. It's giving it that brings us to our center, our soul place, our place where God dwells within.

Sammy Davis, Jr. was coming to Dallas. He was doing two concerts at the Music Hall at Fair Park. The tickets had sold out within a day and even though the concert didn't need any publicity, Canada Dry bottlers was sponsoring his tour. They called and asked if I'd like to bring a film crew to the Music Hall between his shows and grab an interview. Yes, of course I would because we could get it on the air the next morning.

The first show started at eight o'clock in the evening and I had a front row seat. The audience was restlessly

awaiting the first blast of music, then the warm up act
(which I don't remember). A woman sitting next to me
remarked that when Sammy finally came on he probably
wouldn't do a long show because he had another one to do
at ten. He'd really have to save his voice to give equally to
both audiences. The second show crowd had been standing
in line since the first one began. So the pressure on him was
tremendous. Then, without much fanfare he appeared. The
way he smiled, the way he moved, the sound of his mellow
and mournful voice reminded all of us why he had lasted
and resurged all these years. He was energized by our
applause and recharged us by his grace and his rhythm. He
toyed with us through his tap shoes, and we glided with
him as if we were airborne, through *Bo Jangles* and *What
Kind of Fool Am I.* He just kept going, and going. I looked
at my watch and realized that he had been on stage for an
hour and a half.

Then, he walked down to the front of the stage and
hushed the orchestra. He silenced the audience with a wave
of his hands and a finger to his lips and taking his time, he
said, "We have lost a member of our family. We have lost
our brother Jimmy Hendrix, our music making soul brother,
to a Drug Overdose. It is a stupid way to die!" There was
not a sound in the 3,000 seat auditorium. Then, he spoke to
the young people, "The brothers who think it's cool to do
drugs." He was emotional and barely able to control his
tears. He was a gentle, strong, honest, good man trying to
prevent the wasting of young life to addiction! He spoke of
the gift of life and our duty to live it well and proudly. He
spoke of opportunity for all and the responsibility required
in order to achieve. He talked to the poor and the affluent,
the young and the old, the black and the white. He talked
about his love of our country and our obligation to be the
best we could be, not just for ourselves but for our mothers
who cry when we sink down in shame and rejoice when we
stand tall in honor.

When he finished, we just sat in silence. Then, a few people stood and others followed and slowly the sound of clapping and cheering overtook the small little man standing in the spot light. I was crying, the woman to my left was too, as well as the bank president behind me. Together we made the music of acceptance and appreciation fill the hall. We were, at once, "one voice," and one great friend to Sammy. He had done more than entertain us. He had inspired us to be better and to do better. He had united us as "one people" and we knew it. He finished his concert and I realized that it was ten — time for his next show to begin. He had given everything he had to us and I wondered how he could have anything left to give for another two hour show. I was also sure that I would not get to do the interview because he certainly would need a little rest time. I certainly did. I was just exhausted emotionally.

As the audience filed out of the theater, I made my way back stage to the green room where we had set up to do the interview. He was surrounded by fans who wanted to meet him and shake his hand. He signed autographs and posed for pictures. He was never impatient or abrupt. He just gave more of himself than I had ever seen anyone do. His manager motioned for me to step inside the green room and take my chair for the interview. I said, "Do you mean he still wants to do it?"

Absolutely," he replied. Doug Freeman, my cameraman, and I just looked at each other. We couldn't believe this whole experience.

Within minutes, Sammy Davis, Jr. walked into the room. He spied me and said, "Are you Suzie?"

I said, "Yes sir, Mr. Davis. I realize how pressed for time you are, we won't take but a few minutes."

He said, "No, you don't have to hurry. After all, you were kind enough to wait for me. You take all the time you need."

For the next twenty minutes, we talked about everything! We talked about drugs and addiction, responsibility and dedication, Frank Sinatra, Sammy's marriage to Mae Britt, America's reaction, about his fame and life, while the second show audience stomped their feet waiting for him to go on. Finally, I said, "You've got to go, but I will never forget you or this evening. Thank you for what you've given me. Thank you for what you've given all of us."

As we got up, I noticed my husband, Ken Humphreys, standing in the doorway. I motioned to him to come in and I said to Sammy, "Mr. Davis, this is my husband, Ken Humphreys."

Sammy said, "Hey man … I hope you don't mind," and he put his arm around my waist and kissed me on the cheek! I returned the kiss to Sammy.

As I did, the picture of Harry Belafonte and Petula Clark flashed in my mind, and suddenly, everything was just so clear. I understood what it meant to care about or deeply love someone because you just can't help yourself! I will never forget how much I loved and learned from that talented, generous, wonderful human being, Sammy Davis, Jr.

The *Course In Miracles* says, "The holiest spot on earth is where an ancient hatred has turned to love." We waste so much of our precious time in stupid judgments and prejudices. So much energy is consumed by hatred and fear of others. When we are able to rise above that and just decide to "live and let live," our self imposed shackles drop away and we are lighter, and freer than we have ever been. When I've allowed myself to be more tolerant and accepting of others, I have just learned to do the same thing for myself. I owe that feeling to the gift of being able to spend an evening with Sammy Davis, Jr.

Suzie and Muhammad Ali

Suzie's Yellow Van

She traveled the streets of Dallas/Ft. Worth broadcasting on the airwaves of KVIL radio

Chapter 8

I Think Of Betty

All experience is an arch to build upon.
                                        – Henry Adams

Everybody said I had the best job in Dallas — a two-hour-and-twenty-minute job, no less! A job that had no job-description, no supervisor, no Monday morning meetings and I didn't even have to wear makeup or panty hose. What more could anyone ask for? Oh, and I forgot to mention that every two weeks I went into the office and picked up a healthy check.

For my radio show, all I had to do was show up at the station at six-fifteen in the morning, climb into my little yellow mini-van, make sure my radio equipment was working, and sign on the air at six thirty with a cheerful "Good morning" to my long-time radio partner, the master of the North Texas airwaves, Ron Chapman. The job was anything but work It was a spontaneous on-the-edge event that happened five days a week and captured a sophisticated listening audience who like to begin their workday with laughter and an occasional "touchy-feely" moment.

The chemistry between Ron and me happened the first unrehearsed moment we went on the air together. We had a rhythm of banter that complemented each other. We thought alike and subconsciously seemed to know in what direction the other was headed. We knew when to plow forward or shut up. It was instinctive! It was not something that could be learned, only experienced. It was something one either had or didn't. We never questioned the gift, we were simply grateful to have been given it.

I became somewhat of a celebrity traveling the back roads and expressways of Dallas and Fort Worth. Carpooling my son and his classmates during "morning drive" made me like all of the thousands of other moms getting their kids off to school, yet different in that I did mine on the job and over the radio. I became fascinating to other women who wanted to ride with me in the mornings and watch me drive through Dunkin Donuts and pick up a dozen chocolate glazed ones for the kids, drop off the cleaning, stop by my hairdressers for a quick blow-dry behind the wheel of the van, and do all of this while talking intermittently on the radio. What a woman! What a job!

It became a natural progression to offer "free rides in the yellow van with Suzie" for fund-raising events. This extravaganza would be auctioned to the highest bidder, and the winner could bring up to four friends and make the morning rounds with me. This was the case one November when two sisters arrived in the early dawn hours to spend 120 minutes with me on the road and on the air.

The tall sister and I bantered back and forth during the first hour while the shorter sister sitting in the rear seat was silent for most of the trip. When she finally did speak, her words affected my whole attitude for the next three weeks. She leaned across the seat toward me and said, "I saw you speak at the National Speakers Association Convention in Palm Springs, and you were real cute!" Cute? Cuuuute? Cute was not what I was looking for. Fabulous would have been nice. Unforgettable ... fantastic ... anything but "cute." Because she was also a motivational speaker, her comment sounded like criticism or even a tiny put-down. I blew it off even though it secretly confirmed my fears that maybe I wasn't as much in demand as other speakers were. To add fuel to my already festering paranoia she added, "Well, my next year is already booked solid!" I felt the air slowly going out of my body. I began to slump forward so that my stomach brushed the wheel of the van. A voice inside my head said, *"See, your career is slipping! You only have twelve jobs booked for next year!"* I responded in my fakiest smiley voice, "That's terrific!" and kept driving. Ron called me on the radio and our happy dialogue diffused my panic for the moment.

The morning show signed off and I pulled into the station. The two women thanked me for the nice time and I told them it was great having them along with me. The motivational speaker sister said, "I'm asked by my clients to recommend other women speakers who are good and frankly, I just don't know many. So many of them compromise their fees, and I personally never go out for less than $10,000 a job!" *There it is! Proof I was a flop! A small time wannabe not even good enough to be recommended, much less earn that kind of money!* "Bye, Bye. Thanks for coming." *(Laugh heartily, don't let 'em know you're miserable.)*

For the rest of the day I really tried to shake the negative feeling I had developed. I told myself that the reason I didn't have much work was because I needed to rest and rejuvenate. I needed to "fill up the well that was empty," to pay more attention to my family, to fix more hot meals, to spend more time at Blockbusters so we could watch more movies together. *Lies! All Lies! The phone is not ringing 'cause you're not wanted! You're looking old ... your face needs a good lift ... you're fat and you're not as funny as you used to be.* And on that note, I descended into a three-week decline!

A "decline" for me consisted of letting my hair color fade (and not caring), not smiling (and not caring), and in general not spending one minute of time thinking about anyone other than myself. I lacked energy, motivation, interest and humor! Some would call it depression, but I knew better. It was pure anger, plain and simple. It can almost always be found when we compare ourselves to others.

I muddled through the next three weeks not caring that the phone wasn't ringing. Requests to speak had all but disappeared, and I was certain that I would be fired from my job. I just knew that I wasn't contributing anything to the morning show!

One Thursday morning when I had finished the show, I was driving home and that voice in my head said, "Why don't you pull into that 7 Eleven and get a Snapple, a Butterfinger and a pack of cigarettes?" *(Great! Now I can really hate myself!)* I parked in front of the store and two construction workers walked past me as I opened the door. I happened to glance to the left, and there, standing behind the counter, was this small leathery-skinned woman wearing an orange 7 Eleven smock making change and saying, "Thank you" to a line of customers who had stopped in to grab some lunch. In addition to that orange smock, she was wearing the biggest smile on her face that I had ever seen. It was magnetic. The voice (the guide, the friend) in my head said, "Dummy! That's what you need to be doing ... smiling!"

I don't want you to think that I was cured at that instant (I did get the Snapple and the Butterfinger), but the moment I saw her, I also got the message. That was what I needed to do. I needed to smile! I had not done it for three weeks and I didn't like myself because of it. I stepped up to the counter and saw the name badge she was wearing and I said, "Hello, Betty. How are you today?"

She replied, "I'm just great!"

I said, "Yes, you are and one day I want to tell you what seeing you today has meant to me. I'd like to put you on the radio at eight o'clock tomorrow morning."

"No, I can't," she drawled, "No, I can't, that's the time I take out the trash!."

As I turned to walk out the door, I noticed that I was standing straighter. I was even holding my stomach in! The corners of my mouth had turned up, and I was different than when I first walked in that store. Two hard-hat guys opened the door for me and I said, "How are you guys doing?" They smiled, as did I.

The way I see it is that there were two miracles that happened to me on that day. One was that I pulled into that particular store at that exact time to see Betty. The second miracle was that the moment I saw her, I got the message. I knew it instantly, and because I was willing to see myself exactly as I was, I knew that my life didn't need to change … I did.

Allow me to tell you what else I believe about that time in my life. The phone had stopped ringing because my negativity caused it to cease. The moment that I became me again, the positive me, the one who has always believed that what we need is already there for us, I opened up the flow of optimism so that the phone started ringing again, loud and clear.

Fast forward some twelve months later.… It is the National Speaker Association Convention and I have just stepped off the elevator to run smack into the speaker who had ridden with me in the yellow van. She lit up when she saw me, and I said, "I'm so glad to see you. If you have time, I must tell you about the impact that you had on my life when we were last together." We agreed to meet in the lobby that afternoon. I didn't know how she would take my story. It was important to me that I tell it to her, for I would have felt deceitful otherwise.

We met later that day and I laid it all out on the table about her influence on my feelings of jealousy and inadequacy. She leaned back in her chair and let out this squeal of laughter. She took my hand and said, "Do you know what I did after I left you that morning? I went home to my husband and sat on the bed and cried. I felt that I had just spent two hours with this woman who does it all … is funny, speaks on the radio while she drives and entertains her guests, carpools these kids, and still has time to do these incredible talks all over the country. Look at me," she went on, "I'm not half as good as she is!" We just fell down laughing. We both wasted all that time comparing ourselves to each other instead of being happy for whatever success had come into our lives.

You know, one other thing is worth considering. If we're going to compare ourselves, why don't we compare ourselves to someone who has it worse than we do instead of to someone we *think* has it better? I don't compare anymore. I don't have a measuring stick anymore. I am simply grateful for my life exactly as it is. No matter what state it is in, it is perfect. And when I start to slip … I think of Betty.

7-11 commercial. I'm the one with the mustache and the tuba!
Front row: Bob Peck, Frank Harting, Dan McCurdy, Suzie

Suzie and Josh

Chapter 9

Find the Good in Everything

Don't end a day without a laugh.

– Owen James

Before I was hired for my dream job on radio and after I was fired from the TV station. I felt like I was coming apart. You've read those magazine lists — "When To Seek Counseling: Five of Life's Changes May Be a Warning." Well, three of life's big changes slapped me all at the same time. My firing was a big blow. I couldn't get along with a new TV news director who had been hired. Soon after that my self-esteem took another knock because I was going through a second divorce. My third failure was the realization that I was broke. I had to give up my apartment and move into the spare room of my best friend, a seventy year old, Frank Harting.

But the good thing about hitting rock bottom is that it gives you someplace solid to plant your feet. And now, six months after the triple disaster, things were happening. My life was coming up. I'd been hired for the dream job on the number one radio show on the number one radio station in Dallas and Fort Worth. For an hour and fifty minutes a morning, five mornings a week, I flew over both cities in a helicopter saying whatever witty little thoughts came into my mind. I had a new home and a growing new sense of self-esteem. I was back in circulation and starting over.

Then the best thing of all happened to me. I met this wonderful man. Finally!

He had five children; I had none. Most of his children were almost grown and on their own except the youngest daughter Susan, and Susan lived with her mom. He thought I was fun — because I didn't have any responsibilities. It was just me all by myself. He figured he had been a parent most of his life; and that marriage to me would mean we would travel and have our careers and have dinner in front of the fire place every night at eight-thirty — just the two of us.

We married on October 15, and we figured it was around Christmas when I discovered I was going to have a baby. I was forty years old and I was going to be a mother for the first time. I thought God had lost his mind!

Why would a wise God assign an innocent baby into my care? What kind of mother would I make? I was an unstable person! I had no practice at this. Motherhood was not something I had aspired to. And I'll tell you what else. I gained sixteen pounds the first three weeks I was pregnant! I thought it was water retention.

I gained a total of fifty-six pounds with that baby — fifty-six pounds. I was sick twenty-four a day for the entire nine months. I was sick at three in the morning — morning noon and night — and I was flying in that helicopter! For almost two hours a morning, five mornings a week, I bounced around in that helicopter with nothing to say that didn't sound like a nauseous forty year old pregnant woman being held captive in mid-air — and the audience laughed all the way to their work places — the ratings skyrocketed.

I could not believe I had just gotten back on my feet and something like this had happened. That was not the way life was supposed to be. I was petrified. I was traumatized.

And do you know what I was afraid of? If you are a woman, I'll bet you know.

I was not scared of giving birth. I was too dumb to be scared of that. What scared me was the responsibility for another human being.

Why would anybody want to take that on anyway? I mean if we're responsible, then we are not free. Are we? What I did not understand was that it is the acceptance of responsibility that makes us like ourselves. Saying "yes" when it would be easier to say "no." Lord knows you and I don't have time for one more thing, do we? But when somebody needs us, wants us, asks us, we say yes. And then probably in the only private part of the world we have today, behind the wheel of our automobiles, we pat ourselves on the back and say, "I like what you did today. You're getting there you old fool. You're finally figuring it out."

But I did not know these things then. I just knew I was terrified.

When you're forty years old I learned that you have your baby by appointment. I was asked did I want to have natural childbirth? I said, "There wasn't anything natural about childbirth. I wanted to be unconscious!"

I was so scared on the way to the hospital, I put my hand on my husband, Tom's knee, and I asked, "What if I don't love him?"

Tom said, "The baby?"

And I said, "Yes. What if I don't love him?"

Tom said, "Suzie, you'll love him."

I said, "Why? Love is slow to grow. You don't just meet someone, and boom! you love them."

Tom said, "This is different. It'll happen."

That's what everybody said. All I heard was, "It'll happen." "It'll happen."

Josh was born. The doctor held him up and said, "There he is Suzie."

I said, "How much does he weigh?"

The doctor said, "Seven pounds and fourteen ounces." And I just sobbed. I just knew I was going to have a fifty-six -pound baby. That afternoon, they brought my son Josh to me again. I said, "Nice." Nothing happened. Nothing. Zero, Zip. Nothing. Now everybody was saying, "It'll happen. It'll happen."

Next morning they brought Josh to me, and well … well — *it* happened!

Ta da! *It* happened!

You know It? It's that thing that is so big there's no word for it. Go get on that fancy computer and try to get it to invent a word like that. There is never going to be a computer invented that can make a word like that. Or how about this? How about sitting in the still of night, with a half opened blind and the moonlight shining in and resting on a small cheek next to yours, and knowing for the first time in your whole absolute life about the "joys of the responsibility for another human being!" It changed everything.

So for the next year while Josh was growing to one, his mother, at forty years old was finally growing up. I came to a remarkable conclusion about my life in looking back. You know how you "look back?" Try to find the sense in things that don't make sense or find answers to questions that don't have any answers? When I looked back I discovered something that would forever change the way I looked at life and would forever more take away the "fear" in living life. I discovered that the best things in my life had always come in the form of a devastation! The real gifts God gives us, I learned, don't always come in a shiny icy blue box with white satin ribbon and a label marked Tiffany! The real gifts always come in an old brown paper sack and we don't always know they're gifts until later.

A woman asked me one time, "Are you trying to tell me that you think everything happens for the best?"

I said, "I don't know that; it's hard to see sometimes.

But I do know this ... there is best in everything that happens ... the trick is you have to look for it. The trick is you have to not get so down or discouraged or negative that you turn your back and walk away. But you stay with it and look for the good till you find it ... 'cause it's always there' albeit sometimes very small and sometimes great big! It is always there.

She said, "But weren't you divorced at eighteen years old in Hereford, Texas?"

I nodded, "Yes."

Then, she went on, "What could be good about that?"

I said, "I'll tell you what the good is ... I could still be living in Hereford!"

Getting fired was the best thing that happened in my career. If I hadn't been fired I would still be sitting on television with false eyelashes out to "yonder" and never know the joy of working on the radio for twenty years. A pregnancy at forty years old turned out to be the best gift that anyone has the right to even dream about, much less have. The real gifts always come in the form of a devastation.

So the next time you're knocked off your feet and lying with your keister in the dirt ... you pick yourself up, dust yourself off, toss your hands to the heavens and yell, "I can't wait to see what good's gonna come out of this!" Then, settle back, take a deep breath, and don't work too hard looking for the answer.

One day, it will all make sense to you. You'll understand that it is as if the whole of your life has been righted because of the way you chose to believe and recognize the good that came to you. You will, I promise, tear up in gratitude that you have been able to see it. That you can now fully say,... "Oh, I see it clearly now, I understand at last."

Blessings

Tom Mayo, Suzie and Boomer

Chapter 10

Someday He'll Come Along ...

Let there be spaces in your togetherness.
– Kahlil Gibran

Someday he'll come along ...
The Man I love ...
And he'll be big and strong,
The man I love,
And when he comes my way,
I'll do my best to make him stay.

Those were my words, my hope, my prayer and my lament in the song from Porgy and Bess, The Man I Love. I daydreamed about that love from the time I was fourteen, until He finally found me at thirty-eight. After failed marriages and relationships, big as life there he was. Disguised as a friend, wholly competent and interesting, slightly out of balance with the "normal kind of friend," he was outspoken, open, honest, and funny. Did I mention VERY good looking! He had a raw toughness about him that could easily break into a soft gentle kindness and he really liked my quirky, disorganized, frantic kind of personality. He pulled me out of the deep dark hole I had dug for myself after having been let go from my job, divorced again; and virtually homeless had it not been for the generosity of my best friend, Frank Harting.

Tom also, was going through a divorce; one that was much harder than my "divide the apartment furniture and the oriental rug — and take what you want" — divorce. Not only was he leaving a marriage, but his five children. He was the first in his family to divorce, he was ashamed and lost and terribly sad. He did not know what he would do next so he simply decided each day to put one foot in front of the other and try to get through it, until he could formulate some sort of plan for rebuilding his life.

My seventy-year-old friend Frank Harting was also Tom's friend. I met Tom when I was living in Frank's guest room. Frank's home became sort of a half way house for his friends who went in and out of life's ups and down's. We were fed and nurtured by Frank. He made us laugh when we thought nothing was funny. He made us safe from our fears and sometimes our creditors. He had this amazing calming affect that just kind of melted us down from our rigid worries and self doubt. When we were at our worst Frank was at his best. We were bound by our love for Frank and our gratitude.

So when Tom Mayo came to visit Frank, I certainly could empathize with his pain and, in reality, it was good for me to think about someone else's misery rather than continuing to wallow in my own. Tom and I were grateful to each other for listening, and blessed by a similar sense of humor, we found that we enjoyed each others' company. We certainly needed a friend, each of us, but we sure were not open to anything more complicated. In short, being "pals" was quite enough.

As the weeks progressed into months, living became more bearable and even gave us something to look forward to. I was hired by KVIL radio as part of the morning team with Ron Chapman. Tom got his real estate license and signed on with a small firm. We were coming back and we knew that our friendship helped each of us get up and get going. We sort of motivated each other and cheered when the other had even a minor success. I vacated Frank's guest room and Tom moved into a small house, where he stored the fuselage of his airplane in his living room, along with his tools. I gave him my custom made draperies which survived my divorce. We learned what you really need and what you can easily do without. Writing about this now, I think of the hurricane Katrina victims that have lost everything and are starting over. I know with all my heart that doors will open for them and one day they too will marvel at how they just did what they had to do! Keep going ... straight ahead. Life may be fragile, but survivors are not!

We just chugged along — a friendship growing — until one day, while at Frank's, I was cleaning the kitchen and Tom was mowing Frank's lawn when we happened to look at each other in a whole different way. A way deeper than friends look at friends ... a way like people who are "attracted" to each other look. Oh No! Not again I silently screamed. Chemistry ... baboom. It was no time till I was standing up again saying, "I do," and then, three months later, I found out I was going to have a baby. Finding out that I was pregnant terrified me. And so I turned all that fear onto my pal, my friend, my husband. All of a sudden I didn't like one thing about him. I didn't like the way he snored. I didn't like the way he was always going hunting in the winter time. "What am I supposed to do?" I didn't like the way I planned all the social activities. Why didn't he come up with interesting things to do? I didn't like anything anymore and whatever I didn't like about him, I decided to change. He wasn't about to cave in, and so for the next four years, while our son was growing, while doors were slammed and pillows became wet from sobbing, while words were spoken that could never be taken back only forgiven, we would argue, plead, and go for days in silence. And, finally, I believe because we were exhausted, we decided to try something totally different … we decided to take "marriage lessons!"

The counselor was someone I knew, admired and respected. She had traded her "golden girl model" credentials for an education and promptly became a therapist helping people like us who brought a whole lot of "baggage" into a relationship. She was Fayteen Holman and her gentle but strong guidance introduced us to group therapy. Tom in a group on Tuesday and me with another on Wednesday.

In my group there was a tall lawyer who had had enough of my whining and complaining. Listening to me for one year talk about Tom and what he did and didn't do, had pushed him to the limit! Finally, in a fit of exasperation, he propped his elbows on his knees, leaned toward me and said "I've listened to you for one solid year talk about your husband, and I think you ought to leave him!"

I responded "Leave Him? Leave Him?"

He replied "Yeah because if you can't accept him exactly like he is you need to get going!"

I said "accept him EXACTLY like he is?"

He said "Exactly like he is. Now why don't you think about that for the rest of the night and let somebody else talk for a change! Come back here next week and tell us what you've decided."

You know those turning points in your life? Think about it! The turning point is not when a situation changes. A turning point is when there is a *change in your perception … when you are able to see things differently!. It's knowing that the problem is NOT the problem … it's your Thinking about the problem that needs changing.*

I went away that night and for the rest of the week I thought about leaving Tom. I'd left other marriages before. However, when I thought about leaving Tom it made me look at what I would be losing. If I thought about losing him, I was forced to look at what I loved about him. I loved the way he filled a room. I loved the way he walked, purposely, like he had something important to do. I loved the pace of his step and how I had to double-time just to keep up with him. I loved the shape of his hands, and the know how with which he could build an airplane or remodel a room, or write the best letter I've ever read. I loved the way he took my face in his hands when I have no eye brows or eyelashes and says "You are the cutest girl".

I went to my group the following week and that big lawyer asked "What's it gonna be?" I replied "I can do that! I can accept him exactly as he is.

The lawyer responded with "What if he's always going hunting in the winter time?"

"Then" I said "I'm gonna stand on the front porch and wave, 'Have a good time,'" Do you know what happens to a man when you send him off and say have a good time? He's home two days early.

In the three years that I spent in the group, I began to change and take a look at all the factors that went into this inability I had to pick the right partner and then learn how to really love and accept another. I learned very quickly that I never really knew what an intimate relationship was suppose to feel like, much less look like. During the years of therapy our marriage began to feel comfortable. We communicated better and had less stress. We were both fiercely independent and we treasured our freedom, but we were closer and began to work more as a team. I had had trouble doing that. I had never belonged on a team. I didn't know what that felt like either.

Tom was not The problem or a problem. He was much easier to live with than I was. He is not complicated … he is not hard to read if I just pay attention. You don't have to second guess him because he lays it all out for you … no manipulation, no hidden agenda. He is frank, forthright and tells it like it is. This is not complication. He was the way I wanted to be. He is a great deal like I have become just living around him these twenty-nine years. I'm comfortable with it. It fits me like a tailored suit.

There is something so steady and good about working together in a marriage. There is something rock solid about surviving the turmoil of marriage when it's young and feeling the satisfaction of knowing that we didn't quit … we kept working at growing together. We have taught each other so much. We have gained so much in deeper love and given such freedom to grow separately as well as together. If you ask me I'd say that the real purpose of a relationship is to "lift each other." When you're beat up by the stress and the nonsense and the politics of "becoming successful" it's wonderful to find comfort and peace with someone you adore who thinks you are something special.

Now, having said all of that we'd lived in Dallas for a number of years when Tom began making noises about moving away. He had become bored with the city and its noise and traffic and he wanted to go somewhere and do something different. He wanted to go "build something." At first they were just "one day" wishes. The kind we all have … the "one day" kind. One day we'll buy a lake house. One day we'll do a six-month road trip and see America. One day…. These "one days" are the substance of most of our dreams and I was all for moving. One day — just not now!

Why would I want to move now? I had the most fun job in radio (I'd been there sixteen years), my speaking career was blossoming. Everyone in the city knew me or had grown up with me through radio and television. And I loved my house! Tom and I had lived there for fifteen years and we had fixed it just the way I liked it. I loved every-thing about it. I loved the flowers spilling over the window boxes and the feeling the rooms gave me inside. I loved the neighborhood and the familiarity of the grocery store and cleaners. The pharmacy knew all of us and so did the Texaco manager. We had identity in Dallas. It was our community and home and it was where I wanted to die someday.

Still, Tom and I would travel to Texas cities and towns periodically, looking for the one-day place. Sure enough, we found it; Fredericksburg, Texas, a small quaint limestone and rock kind of town, nestled in the Hill Country. The lawns neatly manicured, the houses trimmed in eye pleasing colors, the "fresh baked" smells of the local bakery wafting through the neighborhoods. Local shops were filled with wonderful clothes and accessories. There was even an Orvis Store for fly fishing the wonderful hill country rivers that surrounded the town. Everything anyone could wish for as an escape from the high paced drama of city life was there. So we had found the "where" we wanted to go, we just conflicted on the "when."

Funny how "life" has a way of speeding up the timetable. On a cold January night Tom awakened at 2:00 in the morning clutching his chest. Together we bundled up and drove to the hospital nearby in our neighborhood. We checked him into emergency and began the long arduous task of making it through the night in the emergency room. The next day his doctor advised a full and complete checkup so we began making the rounds in every x-ray and medical testing area that the hospital had. Now, when someone you love is in trouble, your thinking shifts. You get off yourself and on to them. You think about what they want and not so much about what you want. After all, you tell yourself, if you really love them you want what they want. I knew deep down in my heart what Tom wanted. When he was given a clean bill of health, the doctor said that he thought "stress" had been the cause of the hospital visit. Tom was advised to do something about that and I knew I was the one who could help him do it. I told Tom that I thought we had been given a wake up call and he agreed. So, I said, "What is it that you want to do with your life?"

Without missing a beat, he replied, "I want to move to Fredericksburg!" (I knew I was right.)

I said, "Okay, if that's what you want to do, I've got a surprise for you. I've rented a bed and breakfast in Fredericksburg for $500.00 for the month of February. Go find your rainbow."

Two days later, with hope in his heart and a smile on his face, Tom backed out of the driveway and headed south with his black labrador, Digger, wagging his tail from the back seat. For the next weeks he checked properties listed with realtors and the newspaper. He talked to people in restaurants and bars and at the gas stations. He checked the tax rolls and the Chamber of Commerce, asking if they knew of anything that would fit what he was looking for.

He was clear about what he wanted: 100 acres more or less, hilly but with enough flat land that he could put a landing strip for the airplanes he loved, and a hangar to store them in. He liked Tivydale Road, it was green and rolling and far enough from town to not be bothered by noise and the like.

As the days rolled by, Tom's enthusiasm began to wane. Nothing was working. No property suited his needs. Some almost did but not enough to make an offer. Then two days before the expiration of the bed and breakfast, a voice in Tom's ear whispered "Why don't you go back and checkout the property that you turned down when you first started looking two years ago." Tom wheeled his truck around and headed toward Tivydale Road. He thought the property was out about ten miles or so. He wasn't sure that was where it was, but the voice, the silent voice in his mind, kept navigating him toward that spot. Ten miles, eleven, twelve and, Bingo. There it was. Deserted, ramshackled, overgrown and no for sale sign on it. He parked the truck and climbed the fence and for the next three hours he walked the fence lines of the eighty-five-acre tract. Hilly and rocky? Yes. But part of it level enough to put a landing strip and hanger. There was no living structure, but there was a one-room tin building that had once been a general store.

As he made his way back toward the truck, determined to find the owner and see if the property was for sale, he spotted a cloud of dust coming from the front gate. A car was speeding toward him and as it approached he noticed the driver was not wearing a smile. It turned out to be Mr. and Mrs. Higgins, the owners of the property who, on this particular day at the particular time that Tom was "trespassing," "coincidentally" were driving out to check on things. They had not been there for months! Mr. Higgins was not happy with Tom for being on the property without permission, but Tom dispelled his fury by explaining how he happened to be there. Mr. Higgins listened to his story and then, after discovering that they knew some of the same people, Tom asked if Mr. Higgins would consider selling the property. He thought for a moment and then said, "Yes, but the only way I'll sell it is to carry the note?" There it was … exactly as Tom had wanted it. Tivydale Road, 100 acres more or less, hilly but level enough to put a runway and hangar, and the owner who would "carry the note," which was a very good way to buy property.

He called me that night excited about the find and asked when I could get there to look at it.

I replied, "Do you like it and will it work?"

He said, "It needs a lot of work, but that's what I want to do."

I told him, "If it suits you it will suit me. I don't need to see it!"

Then he said, "Okay, now I've got one question to ask you. How are we going to buy it and build something on it?"

I blurted out, "We'll sell the house!"

He said, "What? Sell the house? You love that house."

I thought and then the silent voice in my mind said, "Yes, but it's just a house. There will always be another house, because *happiness is not a state of location. It's a state of mind. You can be happy wherever you are, if you just decide to be."*

When Tom and I hung up the phone, I knew that I had a lot of work to do. The house had to sell, but why wouldn't it? It was a wonderful house. It had wonderful energy for the right people. A family, maybe. Yes. A family with a child. Our son Josh had said "sell it to a family with a son, so he can live in it and be as happy as I've been". Within an hour I had scanned the newspaper looking for something to rent and found a condominium three blocks over from us. I made an appointment for the next day, looked at the space, and signed a year's lease. People said I was crazy to do that before a for sale sign had even gone in the yard of our house. I knew I wasn't crazy. I knew that the house would sell quickly, because *I had already started packing!* Within a week our house was listed with an agent and on the market. Four days later it was under contract at the price we asked for, with a couple who had already been pre-approved and who, to make the story perfect, had one son.

Within thirty days, we'd sold the house and closed on the Fredericksburg property, I had moved into the condominium and Tom, Josh, Corey (Josh's best friend) and Digger pulled out of the driveway and headed south to begin "one day." In thirty-three days my life, as I knew it, had been changed forever!

Today we live near Fredericksburg, Texas — twelve miles out Tivydale Road on eighty-five acres. We have a road, an electric gate, a hanger with office and guest room attached, a greenhouse, a potting shed and a kennel. We live in the old general store. We remodeled, added on and fixed a house I adore. We have been blessed by being contented and happy and proud that we risked all that we knew for all that we dreamed we could have.

I think about the series of events and circumstances that were placed in our lives because we dared to jump into the uncertain and unknown. We were never afraid and we never doubted that it would happen. The doors opened to us, the people that we needed appeared and the life that we wanted was realized.

Many years later on a Valentine's Day, I wrote a note to Tom that proved how wise my decision to "take him as he was" turned out to be.

"It has always been my pattern to go "buy something" for a special occasion. I felt that it would be a complete waste of money to do this and the thing that you would appreciate the most is my not buying you a present that you didn't want or need. Besides I don't have a current list of "tools" that you want.

"So I come to you on this Valentine's day of 1999, looking a little tired, a little old, a little unromantic … 'no eyebrows and eyelashes and two blue holes' … to say thank you for making me feel 'pretty all the time.' In the course of our twenty-four years together you have been my guide for adventure, more growth, more stability and more genuine joy than one person has the right to ever even dream about. You are amazing to live with. You are never predictable and always dependable. You are fun and interesting and truly the most passionate person about living life than anyone I have ever read about. I am still amazed that you picked me to share your life with (even if it was the second time around). Here's to more or less of everything. Here's to growing wiser and older together. Here's to the deepening love that continues to grow, and to laughter louder and more often. Here's to whatever it is you want to do next! I'm with you all the way.

"You are still the best looking man I know!

"Love and everything that's beyond."

Suzie

Greatest Show on Earth — Emett Kelly and Suzie. On the left are Don Harris and Doug Freeman.

Chapter 11

There She Was —
One of Those People

Real life means surpassing yourself again and again.

— Fanny Harper

I f you're like me, somewhere in the recesses of your mind you have this dream of an "adventure." Perhaps one that would take you in a Land Rover through the wilds of Africa, or one that would send you across the rails of Europe speeding through the winter night, nestled warmly under European goosedown, in a sleeping car aboard the Orient Express. Seldom do we ever consider the adventure that lies in the concrete and glass city in which we have lived most of our lives. This adventure happened to me in that city which I called home before Tom and I moved to the hill country.

It was just an ordinary day, really; nothing spectacular about driving to downtown Dallas from my suburb home to pick up a packet of papers waiting for me in an office building. Oh sure, it was an adventure to drive on the over-crowded freeway wondering if you could avoid the speeding fools who were convinced that every second lost was a dollar deduction from a paycheck. As I left my house that morning I grumbled over having to become part of the "rat race." Certainly I would have been much more excited had I been driving to the airport to board an airplane bound for Hawaii.

But there I was, winding my way through the maze of red lights and one way streets, checking addresses to find the right building. Luckily, I found a narrow side street unoccupied by cars or people within fifty feet of the bank building and the reception desk where my packet lay. I could retrieve it in three minutes and my spirits lifted as I locked my car door and walked briskly around the corner and through the revolving door of the fortress that protected valuable brains and money. I retrieved the packet and I was out the door in less than two minutes. Easy as pie — no problem. Until I turned the corner, and *there she was ... one of those people!*

You've seen them. Some holding signs that read, "Will work for food, God Bless You." You've had discussions about them, and so have I. And though in the past, I had closed my ears to friends who had argued that a handout of money discouraged them to "go to work for a living," on this day I was determined to not give in to another sob story, or be fooled by a hang dog, pitiful, soulful look. I would not open my wallet! I would simply get in my car and go about my business. After all, today was nail and hair day! Such an important day! I had no time for her.

She was leaning against a painted grey wall trying to stay out of the wind; not much shelter really. She was wearing a faded pair of blue jeans that looked like they had come from someone else's closet a long time ago. Her chapped hands clutched a lightweight windbreaker closely to her. It was not enough warmth — it was no warmth, and she had on a wool stocking cap that rested just above her eyebrows. Her face was weathered and lined. I couldn't tell how old she was. You can never tell how old someone is when they live outside. Perhaps the strangest thing of all was the white plastic purse she hung on to. She held it close to her chest so no one could steal it. I wondered what was in it. Maybe a lipstick or a pack of cigarettes ... or a letter that had found its way to her through general delivery, from a friend she once knew. It was a quick evaluation ... I didn't want her to see me looking at her. We never want them to see us looking at them. We never want to make eye contact, because we don't want to recognize in their eyes something we see in ourselves ... someone we might become ... someone we could be.

I was determined to just walk straight ahead, and as I did I could see her through my periferal vision, just leaning against that wall, holding tight to the white plastic purse, looking down. I kept on walking. "I'm gonna make it ... I'm gonna make it and not give her anything ... keep walking you're almost there." The voices were beginning to grow louder in my mind. "Don't even think about giving her anything. She's just an old boozer. She could work if she wanted to!" Then another voice more pressing, though softer, began to overwhelm the "don't" voice. "Stop!" it said. "Don't walk past her. Don't turn away from a fellow human being in need."

It was almost as if I were back in the twenty-five-cent picture show and those old black and white movies were playing. You know, the ones where the main character, when faced with a moral or ethical dilemma, had two little figures appear on his shoulders. One was dressed in a white robe and had feathered wings sprouting from her shoulders. (I knew an angel when I saw one.) The other had a body suit on with a tail and horns protruding from the hood. The pitch-fork he carried told you too well he was the "devil." Both were whispering in the hero's ear ... "Do" ... "Don't" ... "Play fair." ... "Cheat." It was a cinematic version of good and evil and, just as always in the movies, good was about to prevail. It was as if an invisible shield fell from the heavens and stopped right in front of me and the pointed toes of my high-heeled shoes. *I could not take another step. I could not walk away. I was going to give her something.*

I opened my purse and found that I only had a twenty-dollar-bill. Okay, I thought, now comes the dilemma of giving her the money but not in a demeaning way. I folded the bill tightly in my hand and turned toward her. She did not look up. She did not move. I placed my hand lightly on the sleeve of her faded jacket, slowly put my hand on hers, and slid the bill neatly inside her palm, closing her hand with mine. She just looked at me and I said, quietly, "I hope you'll do something really special for yourself today." She merely nodded her head, never saying a word, and looked down again concentrating on whatever mental picture she had seen in the sidewalk.

As I turned and walked toward the car, my step quickened, my shoulders straightened and that voice inside my head said, "Isn't it good that you were here today for that woman." I felt wonderful! So, happily, I unlocked the car and slid behind the steering wheel, started the car and for some reason looked at the rearview mirror. Framed perfectly in that mirror was the woman ... sobbing quietly into that white plastic purse.

I knew in an instant that I had not been put there at all for that women, *she had been put there for me.* The point was *not* what she did with the money. The point was what I did. And so it goes ... *things can happen to you and things can happen around you, but the only thing that really counts is what happens in you.*

Casa Manana Production Photo of Suzie (as Miss Mona) and Norman
Alden (as Sheriff, Ed Earl) *Best Little Whorehouse in Texas,* 1991

My father, Bill Malone and I and my favorite friend.
Check out the boots.

Chapter 12

The Gift of Time

Regret which is never spoken is the hardest load to bear.

– Bret Harte

A call I received one day, long after I had been on my own, reminded me of my dad after he and my mom divorced.

The person on the phone had asked me, "Will you come and speak at the father, daughter luncheon?"

Stalling for time, I thought for a moment and, said, "To be honest, I'm not much of an expert on father's and daughters. I was basically raised by my mother. It is from her that I got most of my personality. But you know, perhaps I need to think more about the gifts my father gave me. So, yes, I'll be there. I'll talk about my father and me."

My parents divorced when I was four or five so I lived with my mother but my dad was a daily presence in my life. I think my parents must have agreed to a cooperative spirit of civility and decency to one another after they separated. Since my mother worked, my father agreed to be responsible for seeing that I got home from school. Each day, from the first grade, he would pick me up and take me to the place my mom and I called home. If I needed school supplies, he would take me to get them. He would check the apartment to make certain everything was okay, and leave always saying, "I'll see you tomorrow." And I would! My dad gave me my very first example of dependability.

Being in sales, he was always in his car and he could arrange an hour off each day to be there for me. So, from the first day of school, to the day I graduated from high school his dark green Chevrolet was parked outside the school. Thinking about it now, I realize that the one thing I could count on without fail was seeing that dark green Chevrolet waiting for me outside the school. Often, he would invite my little friends to get an ice cream or go to the park and take pony rides. My friends liked my dad and he liked them. Life was simple … ice cream, school supplies and pony rides. Life was calm and steady with my dad.

Life with my mom, on the other hand, was erratic, exciting and anything but steady, or calm. I didn't see the difference then as I did when I was older, that it was this steady, calm, dependable strength that I looked for in men. That was the reason I liked John Wayne and Gregory Peck. The heroes of the movies when I was young said more with fewer words. They took action only when it was the last recourse. There was a quietness … a firmness about them as there was in my dad.

He had very little money. He had hardly any need for money. He wore nice clothes, though he had few changes … he always wore a proper suit with a crisp, freshly starched and ironed white shirt. His shoes were polished and shined and he never went anywhere without a hat, which he removed in the presence of ladies and upon entering a room. He was extremely thin and slightly balding. He wore rimmed glasses and had a small dark mustache. He looked old when he was young … and yet as he aged he never seemed to look any different.

Sometime I spent weekends with him in a modest room which he rented from an elderly lady, Mrs. Camden.

There was never any sign of disorder. There were no encumbrances of any sort — nothing to tie him down, nothing to be responsible for. Just me. He seemed to like having me as his "purpose." I can't remember what we talked about … but I remember always feeling safe and happy with him. I hope he knew it. When I was about three and did not know my numbers, I used to tell him, "I love you six and eleven." That was the biggest amount I knew how to say. I always signed letters I wrote to him with six and eleven.

The last night I ever spent with him at Mrs. Camden's, he said to me "Boog, you're nine years old and you're getting too old to sleep with me."

I said, "Okay Dad." And that was that! From then on we spent our weekends at our friend's ranch in South Texas, or visited my grandparents and aunts in the little town of Beeville, Texas.

It was my dad who taught me to love the outdoors, hunting particularly. I learned to walk stealthily as we tried to catch game unaware on cold crisp early mornings. Dove or deer hunting with him was exciting for me. I'd lie awake all night just waiting for the sound of fire being stirred in the fireplace and the smell of coffee as it boiled on the stove. Once we were on the trail, I'd step in his boot prints, making certain not to break any twigs or tumble any rocks. He always shot his limit of doves and he did it on the wing. He never missed. He could cook the dove or the venison and there was nothing I loved eating more.

None of my other friends dads ever took their daughters hunting. Consequently they never saw their fathers the way I saw mine, never shared the intimacy of those special outings. My friends knew their dads worked at an office, came home for dinner and went to church on Sundays. But me, I got to be with the man I learned to trust and love.

As I grew older, and my life with my mother and friends became more complicated, I saw less of my dad on weekends. He was married three times after my mom and twice divorced.

When my father was eighty years old his wife, Lou, died suddenly of a heart attack. We always felt that he would die before her because she was the rock on which their marriage was built. She was responsible for helping him to give up alcohol. I never knew when I was young that he was an alcoholic. After Lou died, it became clear to me that it was alcohol that robbed my dad of his self-esteem, his relationships, his career, his finances. The one thing he didn't lose, however, was his dedication to me.

After his wife's death, Dad tried to live alone but he fell one day and consequently had to go to a nursing home. I've never forgotten the sight of him sitting in his chair dressed in his perfectly pressed suit, wearing his crisp white shirt and his small brimmed grey felt Stetson hat, holding his cane and watching as his worldly possessions were transported to a U-Haul. He never complained, he never protested, he just accepted that this was the beginning of the end of his life. That frail, heartbroken gentleman filled that empty room with his dignity.

I was six months pregnant with Josh and I believed with everything in me that my husband, Tom, had been sent not only for me, but also for my dad. Dad liked him. Liked him for me. Approved and rested easier that I was settled with a man that he respected and who respected him. As the three of us closed the door to his apartment for the last time it was Tom on whom my father leaned.

Thirty days after Josh was born, I went to see my father in the nursing home. He was not coherent, but talked about his mama and his papa, and his brother, Ira, who had died much too young. I sat with him not even sure of my feelings, because we had never talked about feelings. I would try, but then men his age just held everything inside. Most still do.

It was uncomfortable for me to be with the man I admired and loved in a nursing home, watching him fade in and out of the present. I wanted to bring him some sort of joy or something to look forward to. As I stood to leave one day, I told my dad I would be back the next day and bring a television set so we could watch the world series. His gaze followed me to the door and then lucidly and effortlessly, he widened his eyes, looked at me standing in the present and said, "Boog if I don't see you again I sure do love you."

The next morning, while dressing Josh to take him to meet his grandfather for the first time, the nursing home called to tell me that my dad was dead.

In a meditation exercise called, "Take the one seat," we sit erect and centered in a chair, breathing slowly and steadily and let all of the compassion, loneliness, regret, fear, sorrow or joy that may be buried within our hearts, float upward so it can be recognized. I did that after he died and my awareness of his love for me and his dependability — giving me a strong sense of safety and self-confidence that I passed on to my child — was his contribution to my life. And like the blessed girl I was, I regretted that I had not told him how I felt, and thanked him then, for his precious gift of time.

Tom and Josh

Chapter 13

Leaving Adolescence
At Forty-Five

Sometimes it takes 'till middle age before we get smart.

– Henry Hallowell

Tom and I had made it six years together! Two of those years were spent "testing the waters." The other four, the married four, were spent trying to just stay afloat! We had warily entered marriage counseling where we discovered that the counseling was not about learning to live with each other, it was more about learning to live with ourselves. Neither of us was convinced that we would stay married, but slowly the exit door was beginning to close. We were finding our way as two and it began to feel comfortable. Certainly the alarm bells didn't go off as much. There were even weeks without an upset or an argument or a door slammed. We laughed more, like we did when we first started out.

So, it was natural that I wanted to acknowledge his approaching fiftieth birthday with a "surprise party". I wanted to do something that would make him excited about the passing of "another year," rather than his usual gloom which always preceded and followed the occasion. *He hated birthdays!* You could always tell one was coming, as he would begin to get a little more testy and withdrawn. He didn't understand why. He just accepted the event as something he would have to endure and get through. I thought that a party would be the best way. Surround him with friends, his children, good food and wine, and his thoughtful wife, and it would break the gloomy birthday blues he had felt since he was a child.

His August birthday fell just before our annual camping trip to Creede, Colorado. We had been going to the mountains since Josh was born. It was a treasured time for us, as a family. We would pack up the gear, stow the huge blue tent into the blue van, and off we'd go. Ten days in the mountains ... my favorite days.

Now I had two events to plan — the birthday party and the camping trip. I loved the pressure of getting every detail tended to. I'd prepare the party guest list and menu, and get the clothes and camp food ready at the same time. We would party on Friday and on Sunday it was off to the mountains.

The fifty guests arrived on schedule and Tom was surprised and delighted to see them. The food was wonderful, the wine was mellow, the hour was late and still they lingered. Finally, the last guest left at about midnight. I began to clear away the mess and fill up the dishwasher when it occurred to me that I hadn't seen Tom in a while. I searched for him in his workshop, in the garage and the backyard. I walked to the front of the house to see if he was talking to any stragglers who were still hanging around and I experienced the blood draining from my face and the tingling of "suspicion" creeping into my mind.

WHERE WAS HE? WHO WAS HE WITH?

Stop! I know! He's gone to the 7 Eleven for a pack of cigarettes. That's it! The corner store is closed so he had to find an open store in Waco a hundred miles away. That's it. Don't worry about this now. Just sleep. Get some sleep! You can drill him in the morning and you'll let him know that you don't appreciate this one minute! How could he do this to you and after all you did ... the food, the work, the planning, the thoughtfulness. You're such a considerate person ... poor you. I fell into bed and consoled myself that when I awoke in the morning, Tom would be there.

Dawn came early and I was still lying in a half empty bed in a house that was a mess. I rationalized that Tom must have come home and didn't want to disturb me. I checked his closet and laundry for the clothes he had worn the night before. Nothing! No clothes! I cleaned up the kitchen, took down the crepe paper, deflated balloons, and We Love You Tom signs that I now wished I had drawn on toilet paper. I cried, pulled myself together, and then cried some more. I swore and played out the dialogue between us when he came home. I cried some more. Wait! I'll call his office. Not there. Has he been kidnapped? Should I call the police? Should I call his friends? No, not them. You wouldn't want anyone to know HE'S WITH SOMEONE!!

By noon I was an emotional wreck. Still, I thought, I'll clean the camping equipment and get the gear box ready, pull out the summer weight fleece, and take Josh to the toy store to find "vacation toys" to help him pass the time on a ten hour car trip! We were supposed to start the next morning at six o'clock on our drive to Colorado.

At five that afternoon in the midst of my suspicions, my anger, and my pain, the most calming sensation washed over me. I simply quit fighting and gave up. I remember this as if it happened ten seconds ago. From the moment the relief came, I sat straight up, and stared out of the living room window where I had been watching for his car to pull in the driveway. I said aloud," Suzanne, let's say he is with someone ... what are you going to do about it?" The answer was as clear and unexpected as anything I could ever have imagined myself saying. "Nothing." That's what I'm going to do about it. Nothing! It was an epiphany. A revelation. An instruction from God. It was life changing. The situation had not shifted, changed, nor improved, but my thinking about the situation had.

The truth? I had played this scene many times before in other relationships. I had been me then and I had also been Tom. I had wrung my hands before and I had caused other hands to be wrung. It was a pattern in my life. I usually set myself up to be left or cheated on, though I did not realize it at the time. I just saw poor pitiful me as a victim. This time, this very different time, I saw myself as being partly responsible for the drama, but totally responsible for my reaction to it.

Maybe I thought, he just left in protest because he hated to be reminded of another birthday. I decided for the first time in my life to do nothing! Then, in an even bigger decision, I told Josh that his Dad was away on business, but that he and I had a lot of work to do, because tomorrow morning we were getting in the Volkswagen Rabbit Diesel, and going to Colorado!

From that decision alone rushed forth an astounding awakening. "What somebody else did had no bearing on what I did. I could either choose to be upset or choose to be at peace with what was!" It was such a powerful awakening. I could not imagine why I had never seen it before. Why now? The answer came to me in a very simple way, "Because now you are ready. You've given up the senseless struggle and caught a glimpse of what's offered to you when you choose peace instead."

Before Josh and I left the next morning I wrote this note to Tom:

Josh and I have gone to Creede. We will check in with Frank and let him know where we'll be staying tonight. We hope you are well and hope you still plan to join us. Let Frank know your plans and we'll check with him tonight.

Love, Suzie

I can tell you that the drive that day to New Mexico was as fun and enjoyable as any trip I've ever taken. Josh and I laughed and played games and delighted in being together. That night from a motel room near a stockyard in New Mexico, Frank told us by phone that Tom would be arriving at the Denver airport around three. I said, "Tell him we'll be there."

And we were! We welcomed him off the plane with hugs and laughter, threw his bags in the crammed-to-the-ceiling Rabbit Diesel and turned our car south to the mountains of Creede. We were excited and happy to be together. Isn't that amazing? What is more amazing is that I never said a word about where he had been or if he had been with anyone. To this day I do not know. We have laughed about this over the past twenty years of marriage. It has been a bond in our journey together. Mostly it was the turning point for me toward creating a loving and accepting relationship that has become the most joyous thing in my life.

I have not told this story to very many audiences, but to the few that I have, I have received questions that may be similar to what you're thinking now. How could I not ask Tom where he'd been? The answer on the human plane is this: I had set myself up to believe only one thing. He was somewhere that he did not have any business being. If I already believed that and he wasn't cheating on me, then, whatever the truth was I wouldn't believe it. Now let's go to a higher plane, the spiritual plane. Wherever he was … had nothing to do with me. It had to do with him. If he was acting inappropriately, then he would have to deal with it and get whatever lesson he needed to learn. The lesson I am so happy that I learned from his action, was that we do not have to attach to everyone else's journey. I needed the lesson. I needed to rise above the suspicions and doubt and fear that had created such distress and unhappiness in not only all of the unfulfilled relationships I had had, but in my present life as well. Because of Tom, I learned about "giving love."

There is a saying, "when the student is ready, the teacher appears." Years later I picked up a book in a bookstore that was to become as important in my life as any book I have ever read. It was written by the wonderful Marianne Williamson and it's entitled *A Return to Love ... Reflections on the Principles of a Course in Miracles. A Course in Miracles* is a guide to changing your perception. It is not a religious book but can be a guide with religion. In the section on relationships, Marianne Williamson quotes from the *Course,* the following:

The Holy Encounter
"When you meet anyone, remember it is a holy encounter. As you see him, you will see yourself. As you treat him, you will treat yourself. As you think of him you will think of yourself. Never forget this, for in him you will find yourself or lose yourself."

One final thing. The basis of Tom's and my relationship began in friendship. It was our hope that we could keep that friendship alive in the marriage. As his friend, I would not have questioned him about where he'd been. I would have known that if he wanted to tell me, he would have. As his wife — the "I deserve to know wife," the "your business is my business" wife — if I had asked it would not have been out of love for a friend. It would have been out of fear and to prove myself right. "There I've got you." "See, I knew this would happen." I'll take the "friend" route any day. You keep the friendship alive and the love never dies.

It was several years after Tom disappeared that he decided to explain why he left the party. Both of us feel this chapter would benefit by his explanation:

"Suzie and I interact best in laughter. Our sense of humor is sometimes a bit sick, but always fun. It keeps us on our toes in mischievous competition and believe me, one must be very sharp to stay up with Suzie. So naturally, for

us, the "where was I and what was I doing?" during that infamous absence was the subtle unasked but unanswered question for years. I was not about to give up that "ammunition," which was just too good to lose by revealing the truth!

"Then, years later Suzie wrote this book. Surprisingly, she included this story. Really, she was telling of her reactions to my unexplained, untimely departure and what she learned from it. Before I read this chapter, but after she mentioned that she had included it, I suddenly realized how unkind of me to have sustained what to her could have been a very dark subject. Actually it was not dark at all, but of course she never knew that. So, Suzie, as you now know, I did not do much of anything at all except drink way too much and be alone to reflect on the melancholy of being age fifty! What a waste of time that was.

"I love you, Tom

"P.S. But you'll never know if this is really the truth or not!"

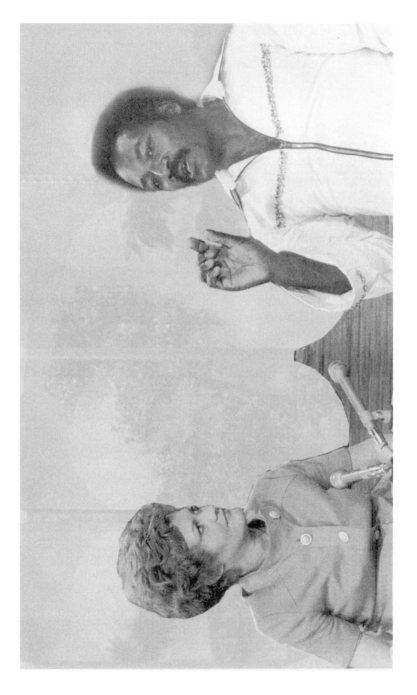

The Great Athlete Jim Brown

Chapter 14

One More Mile

The tradition of trying strengthens heart and soul.
— London Payne

"Mom, there's something I really, really want to do!" our son yelled as he came home from school, barely stopping to put his fifth-grade books down.

"Okay," I answered. "Let's see if it's doable."

"It is," he assured me. "All I need is a new bike because I want to enter the 150-mile bike ride from Denton to Paris, Texas. I get people to sponsor me for every mile I complete, and the money goes for research to cure muscular dystrophy."

"I think it's admirable that you want to raise money, but do you think you could ride that distance? The weather is sweltering, the terrain is hilly, and you're just eleven years old," I argued. "Besides, the furthest you've ever ridden is to the 7 Eleven."

"I know I can do it Mom, and I've got two weeks to get ready," he rationalized.

So, as a parent, at what point do you trade encouragement for sensibility? Do you actually go out and buy a new bicycle for a whim, if it is a whim? Or do you simply provide the "tool" that will ultimately lead your only child to greatness? If you're a dad, you make him earn the money to buy the bike. If you're a mom, it's off to the Spoke Shop!

Two weeks later, before the moon had given away to the sun, my only child and I loaded the shiny new bike into the rear of the minivan and headed forty miles north to the Mean Joe Green football stadium, where some 2,000 adults and one eleven-year-old signed up for the grueling ride. Racing was not the goal of the event; perseverance and determination would be what it would take to cross the finish line. One thing I knew about this eleven-year-old was that once his mind was made up, nothing stopped him. I knew "his spirit was willing." I just wasn't sure about the "flesh."

Josh signed in at the registration desk. We agreed that I would be the last car in the line and I would be on the lookout for him at the ten-mile markers. I knew we were both traveling on blind faith, but when I thought of all the things he had done in his young life based on just plain willingness, I had no preconceived idea of what the outcome of this adventure would be. I hugged him, wished him good luck and watched him wobbly-ride off with the other 2,000 riders.

It was a beautiful Texas morning, but it was beginning to get warm. I knew that in a matter of hours the temperature would climb to somewhere in the nineties. I was glad that Josh had plenty of water, and I wondered how far he would get in that first ten miles.

I let the other "sag-wagons" move slowly ahead of me so that I would be the last car in the line. I was grateful to be in the country, and I tried to keep my mind on its beauty rather than worry about my only child somewhere up ahead. I began scanning both sides of the road. I looked for him at five miles. Six and seven rolled by; then eight, nine, and then at ten I could see the white tent ahead and riders getting Gatorade and orange slices. I spotted him sprawled out in the tall grass. Tears streaked his dusty red face and when he saw me, he sat up straight and at the top of his lungs yelled … "What kind of mother are you? What kind of mother would let a little eleven year old kid do something this stupid?"

"Do you want to quit?" I answered.

"Yes, absolutely," he screamed.

Then I said, "Josh, I want to throw something out and see what you think. Would you like to ride in the car the next ten miles and then decide if you want to quit?" He climbed in the front seat and leaned his head back. Together we rode in silence for the next fifteen minutes. As the twenty-mile rest tent loomed ahead, Josh said, "Mom, I can ride another ten miles!" So, that's what we did, ten miles on and ten miles off for the rest of the day.

At dusk, I pulled off the road and suggested that he stop. He was exhausted and I was becoming concerned. His legs were shaking, and as he once more hoisted the bike into the back of the van, he cried out, "Mom! Can I just once say the S word?"

I jumped out of the van, ran to the back and said, "Josh, anyone who has accomplished what you have, today can say any word he wants. I'll even say it with you." Together, on that lone empty rode we screamed, "One, two, three, S...!" We almost fell down laughing. It was fun "breaking the rules" on that lonely country road. It was more fun to be laughing and doing it together.

When we pulled into the motel that night, he had ridden a total of fifty miles. We downed pizza and Coke, watched a movie and every now and then he would sit up on the bed and chant, "I rode fifty miles." We slept in the next morning until nine o'clock. It no longer mattered to him that he ride with the group. This had become his personal contest. When he finished the ride that day in Paris, Texas, he had ridden ten miles on and ten miles off for another forty miles. A ninety mile bike ride for a first time effort was indeed a respectable distance for an eleven-year-old, and as he crossed under the finish line, he was cheered and congratulated by the crowd.

Fast-forward eleven years: Josh is twenty-two. I'm in Hawaii browsing in an airport bookshop. I come across a card that I knew had been designed for us. It was a silhouette of a boy in a ball cap standing in front of a bicycle on top of a mountain. His arms were flung up over his head in a victory pose. Inside the card read, "Don't ever quit!" I mailed the card to Josh with the following inscription:

"I'm remembering a day in June and an eleven-year-old boy who rode ninety miles in the Texas heat, over Texas hills on a bicycle; remembering his determination and perseverance and knowing how that one single act has enabled him to do so much in such a short time. I remember my pride in his accomplishment and my respect for his courage. I remember how we shouted the S-word together and laughed afterwards. You are a joy!"

I suppose it would be easy to say that this is just a nice story, a mother-son story, or a memory. Actually, as I write these words and relive it, it has become so much more to me. The miracle was that Josh wasn't talked out of this seemingly impossible venture. He was given the opportunity to try. I'm not sure I thought about that aspect of his effort at the time. I only knew that if he wanted to try that badly I just couldn't turn him down.

Too often, all of us are talked out of an adventure. We listen to the nay sayers, and even worse than listening to them, *we believe them!* We have dreams about life and accomplishments and then we give them up because someone else says, "It will never happen. You can't do that!"

Even worse, we often become the discourager. In the interest of protecting our kids, spouse or our friends from hurt or disappointment, we squelch them so that *we* won't feel bad if they don't make it! Being sensible becomes a synonym for being fearful and boring. The truth is, the only purpose in a relationship is to "lift" each other!

Suzie, ABC sport commentators Don Meridith and Frank Gifford

Chapter 15

The Purple Car

*Love is better than fear and faith is truer than
doubt.*

– Alfred Jennings

It wasn't that the car was small, or that you had to lean
over to roll up the windows, or that you had to get the
radio out of the glove compartment and snap it on in order
to hear the news; or that you had to unsnap and replace it in
the glove compartment so that no one could steal it. They
might steal the radio but they'd never steal the car.

Would you steal a car painted a sort of neon orquidy
kinda fushia purple? It looked like a "balloon-a-gram"
car. The two of us would fit together perfectly if I had a
Bozo the clown red wig and a big red rubber nose. My
husband Tom had impulsively paid $4500 for the car to
keep at the airport in Dallas. It was purple and he
expected me to love it!

The purple car, and how it came to be an issue in my
otherwise fun and happy marriage to Tom, had come as a
replacement for a 1987 Volkswagen Fox. When our
seventeen-year-old son, Josh, wrecked an earlier car the
insurance company refused to insure any vehicle he drove
worth more than $3,000. That was the limit he could pay for
a car.

Josh and I decided to find the "perfect $3,000 car." Off we drove to San Antonio, Austin, Waco, and finally, in Dallas, we connected with a used car salesman. He told me he used to listen to me on the radio. He took us to a car auction and found the 1987 Volkswagen Fox for $3,000. We were thrilled. The "Fox" was bare minimum … no whistles and bells. It ran like a fox and sounded like a mosquito when you gunned it up to 60 mph.

Josh did well in the little car and drove it for two years. His driving improved and he upgraded to a pickup truck.

Because we frequently flew in Tom's airplane from our home in Fredericksburg, Texas to Dallas, we needed a car at the airport in Dallas. I had work to do there several times a month. The Volkswagen Fox would be the solution for Tom, or for me to use when we were in town. So, for the next two years we hummed about in the little Fox, saving money and being practical until the Fox began to reach the end of it's life. Signs of its old age became apparent with fuel leaks, motor gaspings, groans, noises and repair bills that grew in size. I began to resist driving the Fox, embarrassed by the smell and the black smoke that poured out of the tailpipe as I entered the valet area of the fancy hotel where I was speaking.

Finally, I just flat out refused to drive the Fox. It was over for me, and for Tom, when it sort of died in front of Starbucks one summer day.

That evening Tom and I met at a friend's house and Tom proudly told me that he had bought another airport car to replace the Fox. I was excited and couldn't wait to know what he had found. After all, I spent more time in Dallas than he did and I thought it was so sweet of him to get a vehicle that wasn't on its last legs. He had a little boy look on his face, and when he is proud of a decision he kind of squares his shoulders and stands up straight and tilts his head back. He grinned and said the car was a good running little Dodge Neon but that there was one little thing that might be a problem. It was purple! I jumped out of the chair and shrieked, "Purple! You bought a purple car?! Why couldn't the little Neon be silver, or white … who in the world would buy a purple car? How can I speak to audiences and arrive in a purple car?

Tom didn't care if the car was purple. He said it was easy to find in a parking lot. He said it looked young and "peppy." I said clients who paid money to come and hear me speak because they thought I was successful, would feel as if they'd been short changed if I showed up in the purple monstrosity. "What do you care what people think about the color of your car?" he pointed out.

"Well, I do care," I stuttered. "Besides the thing that I am maddest about is that when you bought that freak and paid $4,500 for it you never once thought of me! You just whipped out that $4,500 and said, 'I'll take it' because you needed a car right then and there. So now I have a purple car and you have a nagging wife who is unhappy about the whole thing. That's a fair trade off wouldn't you say?"

For the next year, Tom and I would laugh about the purple car. I even reluctantly drove it. I'd talk myself into liking it … saying how lucky we were to have so many cars, and two airplanes — and so what if the car is purple?

Once I got up the nerve to drive the car to a speech in Dallas. I parked it two blocks down the street so no one would see me in it. Then, feeling guilty about being so phony, I told the audience about the purple car. How I was finding the humor in it and how I was trying to get over being embarrassed about it. I even told them that if they would wait on the street when the luncheon was over, I'd go get the purple car and drive past them. Sure enough … 400 people stood outside laughing and cheering as I exited the street, waving goodbye in the purple car. Ha ha ha ha ha hah!

Still, I hated the purple car! When I was in the car with Tom, it was fun! We laughed about the car and whizzed around the city, knowing we would never be car-jacked. We had flown to Dallas in Tom's airplane and when bad weather rolled in, we had to hanger the plane, and drive the purple car home, 300 miles to Fredericksburg. I was afraid our neighbors would see us. Oh Lord! How could I change my thinking about this car?

I came to a resolution about the purple car after reading one of my favorite books, *A Path With Heart,* by Jack Kornfield. The passage that intrigued me read: "In beginning a genuine spiritual journey, we have to stay much closer to home, to focus directly on what's right here in front of us. To make sure that our path is connected to our deepest love."

My path with the purple car is "right here, now, in front of me." That's why I'm still dealing with it. The purple car is my path to humility and I've taken a very long detour. I've been on the Mercedes Benz road. I've been on the "Look at me I'm successful road;" The "I am what I drive road;" the "I want to impress you road." All of those paths were unimportant. I came to realize that I didn't love myself in the purple car!

Some of you may say there is nothing wrong with not wanting to drive the purple car. Most would not blame me for feeling uncomfortable. In truth, however, I admired Tom for getting the car. I admired him for not caring what anyone thought about it. I longed for his courage to be myself, as he is, comfortable in his own skin. I kept trying to be like him, but I was always holding myself back.

The big lesson I learned from my adjustment to the purple car was philosophical and practical. I'm passing it on to you: Look carefully at what's in front of you. It may be a purple car, a professor who wouldn't give you a passing grade because you hadn't earned it, a sister you don't get along with, or an ex-husband you're speaking hatefully about to your children who love him. Ask yourself ... am I following a path with heart? If the honest answer is no, you will know that only love is what is needed to get you happily back on your journey.

And, if you happen to be driving in Dallas and you look over and see me in a purple car, honk your horn to show that you too are following a path with heart. We'll share a laugh together.

Suzie and Robert Goulet

Chapter 16

Life Is on the Freeway

Hold your lighted lamp on high and be a star in someone's sky!

— Henry Burton

S he arrived at her job every morning, punctually at eight, made her way around the boxes and stacks of video tapes and cassettes, sat down at her desk and peered over the mountains of unanswered correspondence and invoices waiting to be sent out so that money would be sent in. She had worked at the recording and duplicating shop for years, and though there seemed to be no logical filing system, she knew exactly where everything was.

She took orders over the phone, appeased the impatient and demanding, and juggled the staff's schedule as if she were assigning landing forces in some war zone, and, all in the sweetest and most gentle voice. A voice that was high pitched and girlish — like a cross between Carol Channing and Judy Holiday. It was the softness that calmed you. It was the crystal clear blue of her eyes and her warm, wide smile that made you instantly know that you could trust this woman with anything.

Her days seemed to meld together. She never went out for lunch, and the only thing she seemed to do for pleasure was to step outside every now and then for a smoke break.

I wondered what her life was away from the "shop". Did she go to dinner or movies with friends? How did she live? I honestly hoped she had a "secret life," some passion or adventure. Some one to dispel the "sameness".

When the theatre tickets arrived for me at the radio station, I thought of her. I could not use the four tickets but I knew how much she loved theatre, especially musicals. I couldn't wait to give them to her and see the excitement on her face. That afternoon I was standing in front of her, pressing the tickets into her hand, and watching her face beam wide as the moon.

She said, "Oh Suzie, I love the theatre, you know I love the theatre."

I told her I couldn't wait to give them to her and suggested that she call three friends, have a marvelously expensive dinner and treat herself as if she were the most appreciated, special person alive.

We were both starting to "tear up" when she looked again at the tickets and then in a flat, deflated, whisper she moaned, "Oh dear, the musical is in Ft. Worth. I live in Dallas."

I said, "Soooooo? That's only thirty miles away.?

She hung her head low and murmured, "But I don't go on the freeway."

I cried, "Why not?"

She then explained that seven years earlier she had been in an automobile accident and she was afraid to drive on any roads other than in a small confined area of the vast city where she lived.

I took her hands and pleaded, "But that was *seven years ago. This is today and life is on the freeway."*

"I know," she answered, "but I just can't do it. I can't go and I thank you, but I can't use the tickets."

There was a firmness in her voice now, a different voice, a resolved and "I don't want to talk about it anymore" voice.

I told her how sorry I was that she couldn't use the tickets and then left. That afternoon I presented them to someone else, and turned my car north on the freeway toward home.

A month later I boarded an American Airlines flight to Hawaii. I was getting myself into my seat when I noticed that an elderly couple was standing in the aisle; not moving … just standing. The passengers reluctantly squeezed their way past them and still they remained frozen as if waiting for something to happen. The woman was leaning into the aisle seat, with an arm flung over the headrest. She was tall, about five-foot-nine. She was trim and meticulously dressed in a white blouse, narrow beige skirt, and comfortable walking shoes. Her tan face was lined and freckled, and the fingers on her hands were long and bony. They looked like gardener's hands. She wore a gold band on her left hand. She was just standing there … smiling.

He was close to her. His face was turned to the side of her hair as if he might whisper something only she would understand. He had a presence that at once was assertive and yet uncertain. You could tell that he had been tall but was now beginning to stoop forward, as if to be closer to her, nearer to her face. He was dressed in a white, crisply starched shirt and gray flannel slacks. His grayish white hair was receding from his forehead but flowing across the back of his neck, brushing the collar of his shirt. He had the stance of authority and I imagined that he had been a busy hard-driving Type A and had either commanded a corporation or a battalion. He shifted his weight from one leg to another and his left hand jingled the change in his pocket. His right arm had been injured and a bandage supported his wrist. He had once been handsome. He still was, in an "I don't believe it anymore" kind of way. Now his eyes watered, and a patch, that made him seem more mysterious to me, covered one. I wanted to know more about him. About her. About their lives apart and their life together.

Finally, a friendly flight attendant asked if she could help them find their seats. The woman, obviously relieved, responded with a heavily accented "British" voice, "Oh! That would be lovely. You see, we're from Sydney, Australia and we've been visiting our grandson in College Station at Texas A & M, and I lost my glasses. We both have difficulty in seeing, so actually we can't read our seat assignments. Would you mind?" He then asked the attendant to direct him to the men's room and then preceded to grope his way from chair to chair, toward the restroom. His wife just stood there smiling!

The American Airlines woman was terrific! She asked at which hotel the woman and her husband had been staying and then a customer service agent phoned to see if they could find the customer's eye-glasses and send them on to San Francisco that evening where they would layover until their flight the next day to Sydney.

When the husband returned, she was standing by their seats waiting for him. He walked toward her and hesitated. Then he touched her face and turned it toward him. She put her hand on his and together they just loved each other. It was a look that no words could describe. It was deep and lusty, passionate and grateful. It was the look of two who had traveled a lifetime together and were pleased that they had made it this far. It was intimate yet unashamed. It was the look we all want returned.

I just marveled at them and, as I watched, my mind shot back to my friend and the theatre tickets. My friend who chose not to go on the freeway! My friend who had settled for day-to-day life in a world that shut out all that was opened for her to receive. She was confined by her own fear and her obsession of safety. Now, before me, a couple, old, half blind, traveling halfway around the world with a faith that what they needed would come, and if it didn't that was all right too.

After all, I thought, it's not life that gets us. It's our reaction to it!

Suzie and singer Brenda Lee had "hairdos in common"
WFAA-TV, 1971, Dallas, Texas

Suzie and Yul Brenner

(He suffered from lung cancer and was promoting "Stop Smoking.")

Chapter 17

Finding Inspiration Unexpectedly

Little mysteries that make you wonder are surprises of the universe to keep you guessing.

— Charles Woodin

I was standing in line at the take-out counter in Newark airport hoping I could grab a quick bite before my plane took off. The picture of the "hot homemade soup" had caught my eye. I knew it wasn't homemade, but it would be hot and quick and having it would be better for me than the Haagen-Dazs double-dip chocolate across the aisle.

The woman in front of me had just given her order: a bowl of soup with two packs of those little oyster crackers. I asked her, "What kind of soup did you get?"

She answered, "Beef barley." For some reason she took the lid off the container just to make sure it was beef barley and sure enough, it wasn't. She laughed and turned to me and said, "I'm so glad that you asked me that question, because if you hadn't, I wouldn't have known it wasn't the soup I ordered. They gave me tomato and I hate tomato!"

Most rational-thinking people would say it was a coincidence that I happened to ask this lady about her soup, but I swear to you that I think it was fate. I don't believe anything is a coincidence anymore. The longer I live and the more I look back on my life, the more I believe that everything happens for a reason. Does fate happen to everyone? Yes. The difference is that some expect it to be this way and others wouldn't recognize it if it slapped them in the face.

Let me tell you about another incident that rocks me every time I think about it. A friend and I had been discussing a book that she had read, by James Michener, entitled *The Source*. It explores the origins of man's search for God. It was lengthy and descriptive, as only Michener could offer his readers, but it was a book that I knew I wanted. The trouble was it was no longer in print and I'd have to find it. I pulled up Amazon.com on the internet, and within a week I was holding the compact blue paperback in my hands. Each phase of man's search, from prehistoric through the Crusades, was fascinating to me, but I could not read the book in long sittings. I'd read and put it down. It would stay down for a week or even a month, and I would pick it up again. This went on for months until I finally decided to take it with me on a long plane flight and do some serious reading. The flight was three hours long, and when I got off and got into the cab that was to take me to my hotel, I did not realize that I had left the book on my seat in the plane.

It is a joke to my mother, my husband and my friends that I leave something everywhere I go. It could be my organizer or my money. I even left my valuable rings on the church sink after services and didn't miss them until two hours later! The way I would explain away my irresponsibility was to say that whoever found what I lost must need the treasure more than I. That is what I said when I discovered that I had left *The Source* on the airplane. Someone needs to read that book.

I forgot about the book for the next two days, and when I headed for the airport, I thought, "I'll go to a bookstore and find something new to read." I walked into the brightly lit bookstore and began to stroll the aisles, glancing at titles that might be interesting. I walked past biographies, browsed through history and stopped in an unmarked section. I glanced up to the top shelf, scrolled down to the one below and then the next and *Wham!* There, directly in front of me, exactly at my eye level with its cover facing out, was *The Source*.

I equate the emotion that I had upon seeing *The Source* with thinking about the first man who accidentally stumbled upon the Grand Canyon. Can you imagine discovering the Grand Canyon and not having anyone right there at that moment to show it to and say, "Look at this! Look what I found!" I wanted to yell to everyone in that bookstore, "Hey, come over and look at this! This book just isn't any book; it is an out-of-print book and it has been waiting here for me to find it in this little bookstore!"

A friend told me about an incident that happened to him in a small Mexican village. He had awakened early and walked to the town square to get some breakfast. He found a little café and sat outside sipping his coffee while watching the birds as they pecked the small bits of pan dulce he shared with them. He felt as if he were suspended in time all alone. As if from nowhere, a band of musicians walked across the street and climbed on a makeshift stage set up under a pergola. They turned to face him and picked up their instruments and began to play. There was no crowd of spectators, no audience, no one except himself and the foraging birds. In that instant he said that he felt as if they had come to play just for him.

I have remembered his story and especially that feeling he shared; a sometimes surreal feeling that the sunset is flowing across a lavender-streaked sky just for me; that the person pulling out of the parking space in front of the store that I planned to enter, did so just for me or that the book I had lost was presented randomly just for me.

There is more to this business of coincidence, synchronicity or serendipity. Perhaps all that it needs in order to happen is my faith that *it is always there.*

Dallas Gridiron Press Show — Peter, Paul and Mounds
Pat Baker, Suzie and Charles Armbrewster.

Chapter 18

So Much To Do,
So Little Time

You're in a rut if you have to repeat no, again and again.

The day was not going his way at all! It was beautiful outside, golden hued with a gentle breeze. The windsock on our small landing strip told Tom that the weather was perfect for flying. "Not this day," he thought to himself. "Not as long as that blasted phone kept ringing and not until the papers on his desk were transferred to the file cabinet. As long as there were letters to be answered and bills to be paid, flying would have to wait!"

I stood back and watched his frustration and realized that the best thing I could do was vacate the office! As I walked out the door, I suggested that he use the rest of the day to do what he *wanted* to do, not what he thought he *ought* to do. "Fly! Everything will still be here when you come back. Make the most of this glorious day."

His response was exactly as I predicted: "Can't ... got too much of this rotten work to do."

I shrugged and headed toward the house.

As I walked down the road to our house, I estimated that it was probably the one-hundredth time we had played out that scene. Tom could not give himself permission to "play" until he got all his "chores" done. His Mama had taught him well. From the time he was barely school-age, those words were repeated over and over during the course of a day, a summer, a spring break ... clear up until he married and had kids of his own. It stuck! "No work, no play! Time is not something you waste." This work ethic was ingrained in him.

I realized that there was nothing I could say or do to change his mind, so I immersed myself in my own 'busyness.' After all, busy is what we're all about. Don't we carry organizers and Blackberrys to prove it? Just look at the calendar. There is always so much to do before we take that vacation. We always find ourselves saying, "The movie can wait; I'll rent it when it comes out on DVD. Right now I've got a pile of work to do." Or even worse, "No time to have a picnic, children. This laundry has to be done because we've got the yard to mow tonight. You know what people will think if the grass is too tall." *Yada, yada, yada.*

I thought about Tom and decided to take him something to drink. Hopefully I would be able to talk him into taking a break. As I walked back toward the hangar, I noticed there was something red, darting and dancing in the sky. I broke into a run and hurried toward the runway. To my joy and wonder, there was Tom lying on his back with one boot propped over the other, an arm bent under his head and the bill of his cap pulled low across his eyes to shade the sun. Tom was flying a kite! In the midst of his frustration and work overload he had done exactly what he should have done; stop and *Go Play!* The kid in him was alive and well!

Play is a very *big* word and works wonders when we remember to do it. When we are caught up in our lives and place importance on the mundane details, we forget to do it so much. Remember play when you're anxious or in overload, when you've had an argument with your kids or you've just hung up on the Medicare lady. Stop what you're doing, take a breath and play. Buy a kite and fly it! Get a ball and bounce it! Tell a joke to a friend and be the one to laugh the hardest. Eat an ice cream cone, a double-dipper, and remember that life is more about living than being busy.

I don't know where I heard this, but it seems appropriate to pass on. A priest said that in all of his years of sitting with the dying, he has never heard one single person say, "Call my stockbroker," as his last request.

Appropriately, from Psalm 118, Verse 24, *"This is the day the Lord had made, let us rejoice and be glad in it."* Amen

Frank Harting at seventy-one, at play in a 7 Eleven commercial

Chapter 19

Living in the Moment

Enough is as good as a feast.

– John Heywood

I t is always an amazing thing to me how feelings (the way down deep kind) can rise to the surface at the most unexpected moments. For instance, the other evening my husband Tom and I were having dinner with friends at an old "established" Italian restaurant. We loved the piano player who played songs we actually knew the words to. We were just laughing away, enjoying each other (I particularly, because I had not seen Tom in ten days). I had been on the road and I was just so glad to be with him. I was rather quiet, unusual for me, just listening to the stories from my funny friends and the background tinkle of the piano. I was totally in the room, in the party, in the moment.

My husband made a comment and I looked at him in the warm glow of the candlelight and this incredible rush of love, the falling in love kind of love, poured over me. I felt like a sophomore school girl with this wild crush on a senior boy. I loved everything about him. I loved the way he looked and the intensity of his gaze as he watched my animated friend tell her story. I loved the way the collar of his shirt brushed his neck and the way his massive hands looked like they could chop a tree or gently hold a baby. I loved the power of his body ... the way he carried himself, the rhythm of his pace, the way he was comfortable with whom he had become and had settled solidly in his shoes. I was absolutely filled with wonder and awe and gratitude and joy for him and our life together and the feeling that I was having at that moment ... in the moment.

Then, without any warning, my mind sprang out of the moment to the future ... the "what if" or "when" future. I suddenly became terrified while sitting there looking at him. What if something should happen to him? He was traveling in two days and I would be on the road again. What if I never saw him again or ... on and on ... an eternity of thoughts and fears rumbling in my mind. I wasn't even at the Italian restaurant anymore. I was mentally standing over the grave site! I had to get myself back to the table, back to the piano, back to the plate of meatballs, back to our friends ... back from my trip of fear to the peaceful sense of joy! Quickly, I reached for his hand and whispered "I love you very much," and he leaned into me and kissed me on the cheek. I breathed in the longest breath of air I could inhale and was again at rest ... at peace ... in the moment.

I have concluded that staying in the moment is the most difficult task we are asked to perform everyday of our lives. It is harder than making the monthly mortgage payment, finding the right doctor, communicating with our teenager, or locating all our tax records for the last seven years. When we step over the threshold of the moment, we are greeted by those two life-long companions ... regret over yesterday and fear of tomorrow.

I know that if I am not experiencing happiness and love in my life at any given hour, I am not "living in the moment." As the saying goes, *"The past is history, the future is a mystery … today is a gift from God, that's why we call it the present."*

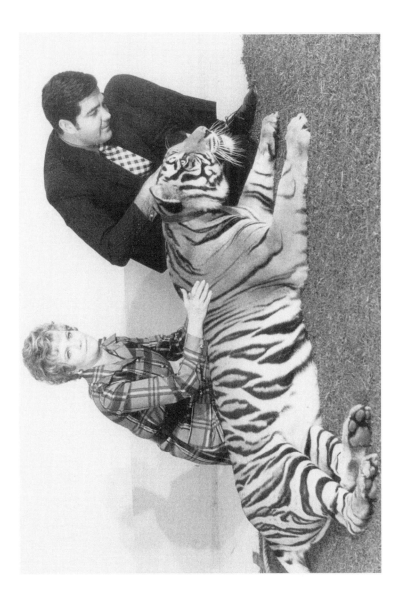

Tabby, you have a flea.

Suzie and the courageous and unforgettable Gene Thomas, my second co-host of the TV show on News 8.

Chapter 20

So, Start Packing!

What man can conceive, man can achieve.
— Jules Verne

I was speaking at a corporate function at which time I mentioned the importance of "living your life as if you knew that what you wanted, would happen." I said, "real faith is buying the sofa when you have no idea how you're going to pay for it." Now, there is a big difference between paying for the sofa and stealing it. For instance, if you have no job and no prospect for one, you don't buy the sofa! To do so would be irresponsible, stupid behavior (like I did when I turned twenty-one). If you do have a job, and are good at it, and you need a sofa, then get one. You'll figure out a way to pay for it. You always have. Maybe it's layaway, or paying it off over time, but when you act as though you know you can, *you will.*

When I finished giving my audience this sage advice, a woman in the back of the room raised her hand and said, "I did just what you said. I acted as though I knew it was going to happen. I started packing before my husband and I sold our house or even had a prospect of anyone being interested." She went on to say that when her husband was transferred to Texas he moved on and took an apartment. She stayed behind in Iowa to sell the house and then join him. They knew it wouldn't take long until they could be together, so they listed the house with a realtor and waited.

The first month produced no interested buyers, as did the second month. They thought they had listed the selling price too high so they lowered it, and still no contracts ... no interest. The summer months turned to fall and the separation was taking a toll not only on their relationship, but their finances. They were paying for two residences and by now were totally despondent over the decision to relocate.

On a Saturday night of approaching winter, the woman awoke at two in the morning, sat straight up in bed and said, "That's it! I need to start packing. It was like a revelation. It came in the middle of sleep and spoke to her conscious mind and what was even bigger, she believed it! She jumped out of bed and pulled the attic stairwell down to retrieve the empty boxes from their last move and, in her cozy flannel nightgown, began to pack their books. By the time her husband called the next afternoon, she had amassed more boxes and newspapers and tissue for the treasures and had finished half of the house. When he asked what she was doing, she simply responded, "I'm packing." He happily asked if they had sold the house and she retorted, "Not yet, but now we're going to."

One week later the realtor appeared at the front door and, with a young couple in hand, asked if they could see the house. She apologized for not making an appointment but the couple was only going to be in town for two days and they needed something immediately. They inspected the boxed up dwelling, turned to the realtor in front of the owner and said, "We'll take it! The only catch is that we need it now." Our heroine, in the midst of her laughter, responded, "No problem, just give me two days and it's yours."

When she finished her story everyone in the audience applauded her daring, but some saw absolutely no correlation between her packing and the house selling. It was a coincidence, they said. You can't make something like that happen just because you act like it will. If you could we'd all be millionaires by now. I simply responded with "how do you know?"

Eric Butterworth, the wonderful author and Unity Minister, shared a formula with his audience that correlates to the "packing theory." It is C+B=A; *"If you can conceive it in your mind, believe it in your heart, you can achieve it in your life. Conceive+Believe=Achieve. Then, you must act as if you know it will happen!"*

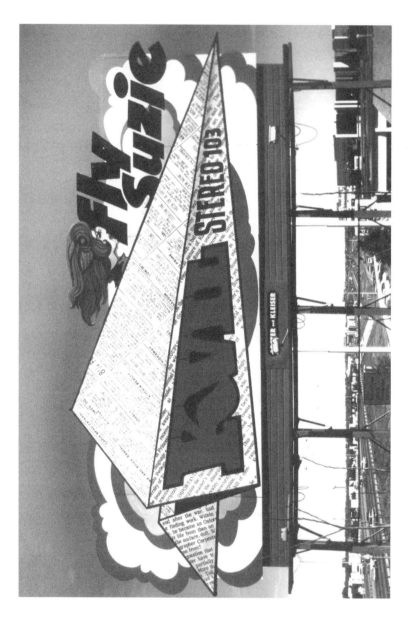

Dallas/Ft.. Worth Billboard — KVIL — in the early Seventies

Chapter 21

Getting Up
When You're Feeling Down

*I've made a great discovery. What I love belongs to
me. And even though I share it, it is mine.*
— Elizabeth Bisesco

Our twenty-one-year-old son telephoned me early one
morning and rapidly fired out these instructions:
"Mom! I need you to listen to me. I don't need you to do
anything. I don't need you to fix it and I don't want you to
motivate me! I just need to blow." Then for the next thirty
seconds he erupted over the phone. I have always given him
my ear when he needed to unleash. Sometimes his
"unloading" was not only at me; it was about me.

For the next minute I listened to him bemoan the fact
that he was only twenty-one years old and was trying to sell
million-dollar houses.

"Nobody takes a twenty-one-year-old seriously," he
wailed. "It doesn't matter what you know; it only matters
how old you are, or nobody will listen. Here I am, trying to
iron my stupid sweat-stained shirt 'cause I don't have a
dollar to get it laundered. I'm broke and don't see any
chances for making any real money in the next five years!"

The tirade went on until finally there was a gasp for
breath, a moment of silence, and then, "Well, that's it. I just
needed to get it off my chest. I feel better now."

I told him that it sure sounded like he had one common thread running through all of his complaints, but I knew he didn't want me to fix anything or motivate him.

"Okay," he relented. "I'd be interested in knowing what you think."

I mustered my courage and said, "You're really into yourself, aren't you?"

He replied weakly, "Yeah."

"Well," I told him, "you know how we all get. When one thing goes wrong, we have a tendency to think everything's wrong. 'I hate my job. I'm going home and get a divorce!' One sure way I know when my thinking is messed up is when I realize that all of my thoughts are focused on me. Tell you what! Why don't you finish ironing that shirt, put on your good suit, take a look at yourself in the mirror (you're a great looking guy), and sometime this morning go turn this day around. Sometime today go do something nice for somebody!"

He had calmed down by this point and told me that he always felt better about himself when he helped somebody else. We said goodbye and hung up the phone.

Nine hours later my tired, but uplifted, son called to tell me about the amazing day he had. He related how his morning had changed when he was stopped at a red light just as a homeless man dropped his garbage sack full of bottles and cans. Without thinking he jumped out of the car and helped the stranger pick up his scattered treasure. Together they tidied up the debris, shook hands and wished each other good luck.

Josh said, "When I got back in my car I felt great, I was totally different! In four minutes of helping somebody else, I had shifted my whole attitude from poor me to feeling great about everything. That's really powerful stuff. I'm going to remember the feeling that comes when I do something that really makes me proud of myself ... helping others."

I've heard it said, and believe it, that what one person experiences, he experiences to teach the rest of us. It is also said that when the student is ready, the teacher appears. I wondered about the homeless man. I wondered if he knew the impact he had on a young man when his sack gave way and he accepted a helping hand from someone who had the time to give. I wonder if that man knew then that one day this story would be told to people who understand the power of giving. I wonder too if my son realized that it was the homeless man who *helped him* learn the lesson.

As it is said, *"We are all students and teachers at the same time."*

The Hotel Limpia, Fort Davis, Texas owned by Joe and Lana Duncan.

Chapter 22

Off to Fort Davis

New writers have a terrible time coming out of the bushes.

— J. Frank Doblie

I knew I'd never get my book written at home. There were too many interruptions and no place to hide from the telephone calls that I was afraid to miss. I had bought into the "bit" that if you couldn't be found immediately, you'd miss the job. They would never call back. I don't know how I existed without my cell phone, or my pager number, or reminders on my Palm Pilot. Forget the fact that if we could be convinced by the manufacturers of how vital they were to our daily subsistence, every red blooded American would "buy" one. The communications industry is rich because they convinced us that what they made WE NEEDED!

The mountains of Colorado were too far, and New Mexico was too crowded in the summer. The place that called to me, promising solitude and inspiration, was only five hours away. So I packed my nondescript clothes, books, papers, laptop and a crock pot (to save money on food), and turned west to the Davis Mountains in Texas. I had once visited the Limpia Hotel in Ft. Davis and I knew then, that it was the place where I could write.

The screened door to the lobby squeaked when I opened it and slammed shut when I let it go. The creaky hard wood floors, cushioned by thick plush rugs, were once walked upon by Texas marshals and settlers who had come here to begin their ranches or careers in a town that was surrounded by desert mountains and canopied by an electric blue sky and billowy clouds. No one was in a hurry, then or now. There was one phone in the main parlor and if you connected to the internet, fifty-seven guests had to wait 'till you signed off to use the phone. The Highway Patrol waved at you as he passed by and the massage lady worked over you on a table set up in a spare room at the Chamber of Commerce.

The rooms were welcoming and better than most where I had stayed. The mattress was firm and easy to sleep on. The bed linens were custom made in vintage fabrics, and the reading lamp was positioned above the head of the bed so that the light fell just perfectly on the book you couldn't put down. The shower above the old fashioned claw tub, was warm and easy, like standing under a summer rain. The small dining room was always crowded and people stood in line because they'd heard about the thin, light biscuits that were tinged with honey and passed hot and often during the meal. It was perfect. It was presented as a gift to the travelers who took refuge here, a gift lovingly given with attention to detail and the joy of surprise.

I set up the laptop on a drop-leaf table in the kitchen and got familiar with my new portable printer. I stacked the index cards, books I wanted to reference (Windows for Dummys on top), turned on the computer, waited for the blue screen, scrolled up to "File," and clicked onto New, whereupon a blank page appeared. I placed my hands on the keyboard and … what?

I'm not a writer. I'm a speaker!

What am I doing here?

I had left my confidence as a writer at home and brought doubt and fear instead. As I stared at the blank screen and waited for inspiration, as I waited for the structure of the story, or at least the idea of one to roll from my mind to my fingers to the keyboard, as I waited, and waited, I decided instead to eat! On my way to the dining room I just happened to meet the owner of the Limpia, Joe Duncan. It was easy to share with Joe, my praise of the hotel; how much I enjoyed my room, how good the biscuits were. Before I knew it we settled into a conversation about how he and his wife, Lana, had come to own and restore the hotel and give it its new face.

Before I knew it, I found the inspiration I was looking for. Joe had grown up in Ft. Davis in the shadow of the hotel. It had been in his family for years. He waited tables, tended bar, painted the walls and fixed the plumbing. Lana's parents had visited Ft. Davis and met the Duncans. They became friends, as did Joe and Lana. She worked in the hotel and it was there that the two fell in love and began to plan their future.

When they graduated from high school, they headed to Dallas, saying "adios" to small town life and hello to "Big D", college and marriage. Joe went into real estate, Lana into education and as Joe started out his career, she supported both of them. Joe struggled in the real estate market, the bottom had dropped out and he was not making a living at all. Still they were getting by until, one day, Joe had a chance encounter. He was in an elevator with the guru of commercial real estate in Dallas. Joe introduced himself and asked if he could make an appointment with the man.

"Look son, I'm a busy man, come see me when you've got something to talk about." Two weeks later, on the same elevator, the two met again. "Look, all I'd like is ten minutes, that's all ... just ten minutes of your time".

"Okay son, call my office and make an appointment."

In his office, days later, the man asked Joe three questions: "How long have you been in the business? How many clients do you have? How much money have you made?"

Without blinking an eye, Joe answered, "Five years, zero and zero."

The man hired Joe on the spot. He realized that Joe had the quality that absolutely guarantees success. He never quit!

He never gave up! All that he needed was better training. The man knew he had a winner in Joe. He was right! Look at Joe and Lana today!

During a successful career with the Henry S. Miller Company in Dallas, on a thanksgiving vacation, Joe and Lana came home to Ft. Davis. With them they brought a friend and his wife. He was Joe's coworker. Joe, Lana and the couple had been talking about real estate investments. The Duncans wanted to branch out and do something on their own … to build something. During the holiday they took their friends around the small town and stopped in front of the old Limpia hotel. It had seen glory days, but they had gradually faded. All the lights had gone out in the windows, the closed sign hung on the front door. Half-hearted attempts to make it go had been failures. It was an albatross around the necks of the Duncan family.

Joe's friend said "Listen, you've been looking for something and it's been right under your nose all along. This should be your investment. This is where you need to build. Come back to Ft. Davis and re-make this hotel. It can serve all the travelers who are discovering the area. Make it something special. This is a hot property and the timing is perfect."

When Joe broached the family about buying the hotel they turned him down! They weren't about to let the youngest brother lose his shirt on the property. Every other attempt had failed. They were sure this would too. They didn't know Joe. There was that quality of his, the never quit, never give up quality!

Well, he finally wore the family down. The hotel was sold to Joe and Lana.

Now here comes part two of finding that inspiration I was looking for right under my nose. If it is true that "unto every time there is a season and that everything old is new again," then the season of the "renewed" Limpia Hotel is now — came to be, under the hands Joe and Lana. They started with one room and made it habitable, and in succession, all the rooms were refurbished within a year. The cash register was ringing up sale after sale. The Duncans paid off their loan to the family and within two years this ordinary couple has achieved extraordinary success through their hard work and willingness to risk their energy, their vision, and their money for a dream. I'm sure there were moments when they thought they were insane. I'm sure their faith wavered from time to time, but they just kept on hammering and painting, living their lives in preparation for the crowds of strangers who did show up, fascinated by the Ft. Davis historical area bordering on the Big Bend National Park.

So, when their dream was accomplished, did the Duncans settle into an easy safety zone of same routine every day? That would have been too predictable for them.

Waking up one ordinary morning, the couple decided to take the day off and head twenty miles down the road to Marfa, Texas, sister town to Ft. Davis. There was going to be an auction of the old vacated, boarded up El Paisano Hotel. In it's heyday, it was legend. Why Rock Hudson, Elizabeth Taylor, James Dean and the cast of Giant had stayed there while the movie was in production. Great parties of notable guests had crossed the elaborately Mexican tiled threshold of the lobby and booked suites and rooms for their entourage of servants and family members and groupies that appeared whenever they heard that a "party" was about to begin. Built in the 1930s it was the fanciest "watering hole" in far West Texas. Stories of "New Yorkers" spending money on fancy food and champagne and cowboy boots made the weekly Marfa paper. The El Paisano was like nothing West Texas had ever seen before. But the grand hotel fell victim to financial ups and downs and, from a swanky private hotel, was converted to a time share property with over 800 members scattered all over the world. Soon bankrupt, broken-down and busted flat, the boarded up Paisano became the ghostly reminder of a happier time. When the Duncans visited, it was a blight on Main Street, which, itself became only a memory of a more prosperous time. Everything in Marfa seemed to have shut down, except for Carmen's Café where you could still get the best Mexican Food within 200 miles.

On the day of the auction, Marfa was limping along with a real estate company, a couple of attorneys, gas stations, two bars, several churches, and a fabulous court house not fully occupied. As the Duncan's were driving the long, perfectly straight highway, Lana blurts out "Why aren't we bidding on the Paisano?"

Joe jerked so hard the car swerved and as he was trying to straighten it out again he cried "Lana, are you crazy? We can't buy the Paisano. First off we don't have the money. It would take a huge amount of remodeling and, besides, you see that jet airplane over there on the Marfa Airport?"

"Yes I see it, Joe"...

"Well it belongs to a rich Texas man who's come here to buy the hotel; luckily, we will not be buying any real estate today!"

Now, here's where the story gets really interesting. Little did Joe and Lana know, but only the night before, the wife of the owner of that jet airplane, convinced her husband that the last thing she wanted to do was start a project like resurrecting a dilapidated hotel; grand as El Paisano was in the past, it had no future in their lives.

As the Duncans approached the auction site, said hello to the town regulars and mingled with new visitors, Lana sidled up to the bidding sheet and found that the rich man had removed his name from the list. The auctioneer with gavel in hand opened the bidding at $155,000 which was owed in back taxes. Little Lana just lifted up her hand signifying that she was in for that amount. Another hand went up in the crowd, raising the bidding to $160,000. Lana, undaunted went up to $170,000 while Joe went down on his knees. All he thought he was doing an hour earlier was "going" to the auction; he never figured he'd be in it. One more counter bid from the stranger in the back and a final bid came by Lana. They'd bought the old hotel for $185,000.

There was applause, congratulations, and the crowd dispersed, leaving Joe and Lana together to figure out where were they gonna get $185,000 cash money by two that afternoon. It was Saturday and they discovered that the officers and directors of their bank were all on a banking convention in Las Vegas. Now what? All their dealings had been with the bank in Ft. Davis. They had a great track record and they had no banking history with anyone else in Marfa or even Alpine, twenty-five miles away. Luckily, everybody knows everybody in the small towns in far West Texas, so a couple of telephone calls yielded the name of the hotel in Vegas where the bankers were staying. Another call found the president of the bank and "bingo," the money was loaned! Okay, that done, what next?

What next? Well, because of the erratic history of the hotel, it was learned that the last owner had sold time shares to the hotel. Eight hundred time shares. So now the title work had to be done by locating the 800 time share owners, or their heirs, and releases obtained. Can you imagine tracking down all those people? But it was done over two years and now the Paisano is the Star of "Marfa" and West Texas. Open and available to the travelers who now come from as far as New York City and Los Angeles. There is a new big artist colony in Marfa and patrons and supporters book the plush rooms at the Paisano. Tom and I love going there.

As I thought about the enormous ventures the Duncans undertook, I wondered how they kept from being overwhelmed mentally as well as emotionally. I could relate in a small way because of the travel and commitment challenges that I faced in my speaking business. I'm asked all the time "How do you travel so much? How do you keep from hating being on the road and away from home?" I think the Duncan's probably did what most of us discover in handling our busy lives: They took one step at a time. That was the inspiration I needed to finish my book — one chapter at a time.

The lesson of the Duncans reminded me of my son Josh's Second grade teacher, Mrs. Dauphine.

Mrs. Dauphine discovered that when she gave Josh a two page test he just froze. So, she only gave him one page. He answered those questions easily, and then, she handed him the second page. One step at a time. I'm a strong advocate of the "three little pigs" theory. One pig built his house out of straw, one out of mud … but the third little pig built his house "one brick at a time."

There are so many wonderful lessons I relearned from the Duncans.

1. Never give-up … just keep on going straight through the pain or the hardship.
2. Don't look at the whole picture … take it one step at a time.
3. What you can dream, you can achieve. It starts first with the dream and don't make it too small. It's easy to bring your thinking down, but it's hard for most people to bring their thinking up!

Next time you want to see the majestic force of the Texas Big Bend country; next time you want to escape to noiseless solitude, and feel an easy style of moving through your day, turn your car West to I-10 in Texas and head to Ft. Davis, Marfa or Alpine. Drop in at the Limpia Hotel or El Paisano, book a room and ask if Joe or Lana Duncan is around.

Tell them what an inspiration they are to folks who want to follow their dream.

The Duncans can head you in the right direction.

Suzie's Special Place
A 10' x 20' room next to her greenhouse.

Chapter 23

Choosing Peace Not Fear

It is never any good dwelling on what worries you.
Fretting makes fear worse.

– Archie Moore

W ell, the bad news is its cancer. The good news is that
it's at zero stage. "Okay! Right! Thank you for
calling. No, I'm fine." I lied, "we'll go from here and just do
what we have to do. Bye...."

"Okay, this is doable," I muttered, as I made my way
to the office to tell my husband, Tom. Bracing myself to
find the right words, I impulsively blurted out, "Honey, Dr.
Diane called and I do have a little breast cancer. Now before
you say anything I'm fine about this I really am, I mean if
Christopher Reeves could go through paralysis and
breathing on a respirator, I can do this. It could be so much
worse."

Tom just looked at me ... partly stunned and confused
at the same time. "Suzie, a 'little' breast cancer? Is that like
a 'little pregnant?' Sit down, please," he said. Then, taking
my hands, he leaned across, and looking at me with those
clear blue eyes said, "Well, here we are. If it's not this, then
it might be that one of us slips and falls on the ice! It's just
where we are at this stage in our life. We are going to get
through this and you are going to do fine"

He was encouraging and he was right. I was going to do fine. After all, we decided to be fine right there and then … piece of cake.

Look at the calendar, I thought. You'll need to arrange your schedule and if you can just hold off on the surgery for two weeks, you can do the six speeches: cancel one, do the surgery on January 23 and be in Vegas on the sixth of February to speak to 900 dentists. It was as if I were starting rehearsals for a play. So, this was what it was like to face cancer. I hoped I would be brave. I could be an inspiration. Yes, that was the role I'd play. Like my friend Kay Russell who had double knee replacements, I would be the best patient my doctor ever had. The staff would all marvel at my good nature and my fearless determination to be an inspiration to those around me. That was the way I was going to play this life-drama out — a cross between Garbo's Camille and Doris Day's Calamity Jane. Poised yet perky.

There was to be a "core biopsy" … something about which I knew nothing. I arrived at the scheduled time and half listened to the explanation of what the procedure involved. It would be similar to a mammogram only you lay down on your stomach on a padded table with a cutout where the breasts would hang down. Then, like a mammogram, the breast would be positioned so that very accurate pictures could be taken of the suspicious areas. Once those areas were pinpointed then a long hollow needle would be inserted by something akin to a "staple gun" and sample tissue extracted.

The needle was the easy part. The tough part was positioning and squeezing my breast. Oh, nobody told me it would be like this. The pain came so suddenly it literally took my breath away, and then I started shaking uncontrollably and crying in great silent waves. I was so tense and in such pain I was frantically fighting to not tell them to stop. I was a baby, trembling and shaking until, in a matter of minutes, I was totally exhausted — and I let go.

If you ask me what transpired in that cold examining room to that pathetic frightened "me" on that particular day, I would say a "miracle happened." And that "letting go" took me to the most peaceful, perfectly calm place that I had ever been in my life. Though the pressure was just as immense for the next several minutes and the pain just as intense, I didn't feel it. When I gave up my fight, I let go of the fear. The pain was still there, but I no longer felt it. My body and mind were just numb, as if I had crossed over the experience itself, still fully aware I was living it, but feeling disconnected from it. I remember thinking that crossing over the pain must be how mystics walk on beds of nails or burning coals.

Afterwards, I told the doctors and nurses what had happened and how grateful I was to have had the whole experience. I had gone deeper and farther in what I call a "holy instant", an awareness of what our minds are capable of doing. I felt totally protected and loved and I knew without doubt that I was given the "peace of God." I had always wanted to feel that experience. I had heard of others who had, but I never expected to find it, especially in the cold clutches of cancer.

After I dressed and left the hospital to get into my car I remember being almost "out of focus." I sat in the car and just cried hard and audibly, not caring if anyone in the parking lot could hear or see me. You know what I'm talking about don't you? You know, how strong you can be in a crisis, fully functioning, thinking of everything that needs to be done, comforting others, preparing food, just busying yourself to stave off the reality of what really is happening inside you. And afterward, when the last guest has gone and the dishes cleaned, when the beds are turned down and everyone is tucked in, then maybe in a closet or some place out of reach from anyone interrupting ... we just "let 'er rip." The tears just flow, the shoulders shake until the exhaustion comes and we slowly melt into the featherbed of peace.

I sat in the parking lot too dazed and numb to drive. And then totally alert, I remembered a prayer I had made to God. I have a special place on our ranch; a ten by twelve foot little cottage-like building that I call the potting shed. It serves as almost a "sanctuary" for me when I am tired, or troubled, or worried. It is like having my own church. I have a small iron bed in it, and a wonderful antique table filled with photographs of my family of loved ones, some still with us and some who have passed over. My special books are there, my soul books, my *Bible.* Favorite art pieces I love, some crosses and candles that I burn in prayers for friends who are suffering, for strangers I see in the news that desperately need help and consoling.

There are no sounds in the room. No air-conditioning motors, no telephones, no compressors, or buzzing from electric lines, just the rare sound of "silence."

It was almost a year earlier when I came home from a ten day trip and I literally could not wait to go to my little room "the potting shed." I was fatigued but happy, grateful to be home again and in my prayer of gratitude, I said to God, in joy, "God, I don't want to leave this life without knowing all that you want me to learn. I am ready to learn it Father and I am willing to learn it in any way you want to teach me."

Sitting in my car after the "core biopsy," I wondered about "answered prayers." I wondered if I had subconsciously asked for cancer as my teacher. Certainly every time I met a cancer survivor, I had imagined what it was like for them to go through the treatments and hair loss and yet to joke about the turbans they wore or not having any eyebrows. Did I ask for this? Since it is a question to which there is no answer, I quickly knew that whether asked for or not, I was going to learn about what I was really made of. Whether I could take what lay ahead with humor and grace, or would I let my self down and those who loved me, by making it harder mentally then it had to be. If I could keep the "fear" at bay, I would do okay.

I called Kay from the parking lot and told her about the whole experience. She is one of four of my closest women friends with whom I have been bound spiritually over the past twelve years. We are closer than sisters. We help each other through everything. We are gently honest with each other and we understand the depths to which we can descend in fear and the heights to which we can "soar" through faith. We have studied and learned and are joyful in our experiences. She cried with me on the phone and I went to change my clothes and do a speech in the afternoon.

The following day I was called by my doctor to tell me that we needed to do another core biopsy on the other breast. Well, I knew what to expect now, didn't I? I told Kay when I would be going and she wanted to come with me. I really do better if no one "hovers" over me, not that she would, but I get a lot of strength doing things by myself. I thanked her and told her how much I appreciated her concern and went on my way.

The following week, there I was again, lying in that cold room, on that cold padded table waiting for that "vise" to squeeze my good breast. Squeeze, it did. But it was not at all painful. We all talked about how easy it was on me the second time, and during the chit chat my cell phone rang. I said, "I don't suppose this would be a good time for me to answer that?" The doctor replied from his little roll-around-stool, "I don't suppose it would."

We went back to random chat, and in another fifteen minutes the procedure was ended. Still half dressed, but discreetly covered in a little teeny shoulder cape, I thought it would be a good time to check my cell phone message. After listening and laughing so hard, the nurses wanted to know what was so funny. So, replaying the message and putting it on speaker phone, they heard this message from Kay:

"Oh Suzie, I feel horrible about what they are doing to you with that old core biopsy. I just can't stand it that you are in pain. I wish you had let me come with you but I know how independent you are and you are so brave. But if I could I would have gladly gone through this with you. I know you're probably out of there by now and I remembered that you said you might be going to Neiman Marcus afterward and I was wondering if you were … would you mind stopping by the Bobbie Brown counter in cosmetics and pick me up a tube of "lip-gloss!"

Oh how we laughed in that cold examining room. We laughed loud and hard and strong and all of us needed that: especially the nurses who, every day, dealt with tragedy and with patients who come fearing the worst and hoping for the best. Kay certainly took me to that peaceful place again. I got there through a different form of transportation, but the results were the same. Peace with what was. Peace, whatever the circumstance.

I did have a mastectomy and I did do that speech in Las Vegas nine days later. My son Josh went with me and ran interference at the airport, carried the luggage and just made me feel safer. We watched movies and had room service and I slept. Then I got up and spoke. Afterward I was completely tuckered out.

My cancer was at "zero" stage. I did not have to take chemo or radiation. I almost feel ashamed sometimes when I see others who have gone through so much suffering and inconvenience. I think though that the ones who do the best, in spite of the pain, are the ones that find humor in the most unexpected places on the most out-of-the-ordinary days.

We are all walking around with an "it" of some sort. It can be cancer, or heart disease, grief over the loss of a loved one, a broken marriage, an estranged child, guilt over the past, or fear of the future. In each of the burdens is an opportunity to go beyond what we think we can do and flourish in the face of pain, despair and tragedy.

About two weeks after the mastectomy I became "voiceless" for three days. I had to cancel two speaking engagements and that had not happened but two other times in my twenty-three years of speaking. I went, that day — as if I had made an appointment — to a healing service at the St. Barnabas Episcopal church. This particular service was always held in a tiny old rock and chink log cabin — the oldest building in Fredericksburg. Inside there are six small short pews handmade of oak, each of which seats three slender people and two a bit heftier. There were six women in the two front rows and on the back left pew was an elderly man I knew as Professor Bob. He was so stooped over his head was level with his waist. He walks from his home every Thursday with his old dog, Hobo, a short haired old cataract-eyed dog with a black ring around his left eye. I sat on the last pew across the aisle from the two pals. During the reading of the scripture for that day, I listened with my aching heart, but watched Hobo as he watched me. We stared at each other as his master, Bob, nodded off to sleep and it was so peaceful that I started to cry. Hobo waddled over to me and just touched his nose to my hand, and his tail seemed to wag in cadence to the "prayers of the people" that was softly whispered by the others. It was the most "holy" instant for me, seeing those two in that little bitty cabin of a church. I started to cry and just couldn't stop. I was still crying as we took communion and then I stayed at the railing for a hands on healing. Father Bill placed his hand on me and immediately from behind me the others came and placed their hands on me. Bob and Hobo came too. Oh! The breath just went out of me again. It was so beautiful that even now, telling you who are reading this, I am crying once again. God just shines a light anywhere we ask for it and even when we forget to ask. I felt that light that day and it still shines as brightly in my mind now. I hope you feel it shine on you tomorrow.

Amen.

Suzie loves this photo by Cheryl Kimple Travis

Chapter 24

Thank You Lord

No line can be drawn between good people and bad ones, when God has not.

— Ethen Evans

I was seated at the head table one night for a meal of barbeque fixed by the small town's best caterer. I was totally unprepared for the impact the preacher sitting next to me would have on me when he got up to bless the food. I was totally overwhelmed by the power of his prayer. It was a real prayer; about everyday things and everyday folks. It was a prayer, simple in words but profound in awareness of "everything" as a blessing. He told me later when I asked, that "Thank You Lord" came from the book *Prayers,* by Michael Quoist, a French priest. I found two copies of the out-of-print book and gave one to an Episcopal priest in my hometown. I don't believe he has read the book, because I know, if he had, he would have sent me a "thank you" note.

If you would like to fully experience the prayer, read it aloud in your special place.

Thank You Lord

Thank You, Lord, Thank You.
Thank You for all the gifts that You have given me today,
Thank You for all I have seen, heard, received.

Thank You for the water that woke me up, the soap that
    smells good, the toothpaste that refreshes.
Thank You for the clothes that protect me, for their color
    and their cut.

Thank You for the street-cleaning truck and the men who
    run it, for their morning shouts and all the early noises.
Thank You for my work, my tools, my efforts.

Thank You for Jim who lent me his file, for Danny who
    shared his sandwich, for Charlie who held the door for
    me.
Thank You for all the life that flowed swiftly between the
    windowed walls of the houses.

Thank You for the food that sustained me, for the glass of
    water that refreshed me.
Thank You for the car that meekly took me where I wanted
    to be, for the gas that made it go, for the wind that
    caressed my face and for the trees that nodded to me on
    the way.
Thank You for the family who welcomes me at home, for
    their tactful affection, for their silent presence.

Thank You for the time you have given me.
Thank You for life.
Thank You for grace.
Thank You for being there, Lord.
Thank You.

Michael Quoist
Prayers
June 18, 1954, Lehavre, France

Slurpee commercial for 7 Eleven — Suzie and Frank Harting
If All Else Fails ... Laugh

Chapter 25

The Last Few Pages

Like epigrams the moments fall;
Do not strive to grasp them all.

– Thorn Bacon

In these last few pages I am presenting you with some thoughts, epigrams, poetry and reflections you may wish to consult when you need an inspiration. They've helped me. I hope they will help you.

If you have heard any of my presentations, you know that I always end with the word of Robert Hastings. It seems that everyone now talks about the "journey" but the first time I actually read his words was at a dinner function where I was the guest speaker. I had done many presentations for Americorp. It is a relocation company that specializes in huge corporate moves, bringing hundreds of employees to new cities and neighborhoods across the country. Bill and Gayle Plummer are a hard working husband and wife team who run the company. They brought me in to help the employees overcome their fears and reservations about leaving their families and friends and relocating to a new town and in some cases a new state, or a new country.

On one occasion, as I was finishing dessert, I was given a copy of *The Station.* I closed my presentation that night by reading it to my audience. I have used it in all my talks since then.

Robert Hastings and I never met. He passed away at his home in Indiana. Every time I quote him, I have this feeling that a little tiny bell is going off in heaven letting Robert Hastings know how many of us he touched during his time on earth.

The Station

Tucked away in our subconscious is an idyllic vision that spans the continent. We are traveling by train. Out our windows we see the children waving at crossings; the cattle grazing on the distant hillside; we see row upon row of corn and wheat and smoke and steam pouring from the power plants. We see city skylines and village halls; but uppermost in our minds is the final destination.

When we reach the station so many wonderful things will happen. The bells will be ringing; the flags will be waving and the pieces of my life will just fall into place like a completed jigsaw puzzle. How restlessly we pace the aisles damning the miles for loitering ... waiting for the station.

When I reach the station "That will be it!" we cry; "when I'm eighteen; when I put that last kid through college; when I pay off the mortgage; when I get that new Mercedes Benz; when I reach the age of retirement ... then I shall live happily ever after!"

Well, sooner or later we must realize ... there is no station. There's no one place to arrive at once and for all. The true joy of the journey is the trip! The station is only a dream and it constantly outdistances us. "Relish the moment" is a good motto especially when you couple it with Psalm 118;24 which says "This is the day the Lord hath made; let us rejoice and be glad in it." It isn't the burdens of today that drive men mad. It's the regret over yesterday and the fear of tomorrow. Regret and Fear are twin thieves that rob us of today!

So, stop pacing the aisles and counting the miles! Instead climb more mountains and swim more rivers; go barefoot more often; laugh more and cry less, forgive always and eat more ice cream!

Life should be lived as we go along ...
The Station will come soon enough.

Robert Hastings

~ ~ ~

Those of you who have read this far in my book, certainly know how I feel about my husband, Tom. Here are some verses I wrote that may touch the place in your heart that is reserved for the love of your life.

I used to dream that I would be lucky
*   and marry a man like you*
You slept in my mind
*   which awakened to find*
What you wish for can always come true.

I dreamed you'd have strength and conviction
*   Give honor to all, not a few,*
There would be no place for hatred of race
*   Or if someone believed differently than you.*

You would be fair and admit when you're wrong
*   Apologize when you needed to do it.*
You would swallow false pride and step to the side
*   Of a friend who hurt and you knew it.*

You would give me freedom and space to develop my place
*   In the world and the life we shared.*

We would stand shoulder to shoulder as we grew older,
        as equals, lovers and pals.

And the kid in you has never dimmed
        Nor the light in your sky blue eyes.
The laughter, the teasing, the fun, the appeasing
        Mark your playful and pleasing style.

So Leo the Lion has grown tamer
        You've mellowed and quieted your roar.
Your strength is still there
        Though the mane has less hair
You found peace you did not know before.

So here's to the next adventure,
        Though the years be thirty or ten,
In your plane or a front porch rocker
        You lead, I'll follow my friend.

Whether we build up or tear down,
        Stay put or move on
Tis not the place that I've finally found.
        It's the dream of a girl
Who's been given the world
        By the man her heart rests upon.

Happy Birthday Tom

                            August 4, 2002, Suzie

~ ~ ~

If you've never read *Desiderata*, you'll be pleased with the words of this writer.

Go placidly amongst the noise and the haste, and remember what peace there be in silence. As far as possible without surrender be on good terms with all persons. Speak your truth quietly and clearly; and listen to others, even the dull and ignorant. They, too, have their story. Avoid loud and aggressive persons; they are vexations to the spirit. If you compare yourself with others, you may become vain and bitter, for always there will be greater and lesser persons than yourself. Enjoy your achievements as well as your plans.

Keep interested in your own career, however humble; it is a real possession in the changing fortunes of time. Exercise caution in your business affairs, for the world is full of trickery. But let this not blind you to what virtue there is; many persons strive for high ideals, and everywhere life is full of heroism.

Be yourself. Especially do not feign affection. Neither be cynical of love; for in the face of all aridity and disenchantment, it is as perennial as the grass. Take kindly the counsel of the years, gracefully surrendering the things of your youth. Nurture strength of spirit to shield you in sudden misfortune. But do not distress yourself with imaginings. Many fears are born of fatigue and loneliness.

Beyond a wholesome discipline be gentle with yourself. You are a child of the universe, no less than the trees and the stars, you have a right to be here. And whether or not it is clear to you, no doubt the universe is unfolding as it should. Therefore, be at peace with God, whatever you conceive Him to be, and whatever your labors, and aspirations, in the noisy confusion of life, keep peace with your soul. With all its shame, drudgery, and broken dreams, it is still a beautiful world. Be careful. Strive to be happy."

Max Ehrman (1692)
Found in Old St. Paul's Church, Baltimore

~ ~ ~

This too will give you insight:

To Remember Me

The day will come when my body will lie upon a white sheet neatly tucked under four corners of a mattress located in a hospital busily occupied with the living and the dying. At a certain moment a doctor will determine that my brain has ceased to function, and that, for all intents and purposes, my life has stopped. When that happens, do not attempt to instill life into my body by the use of a machine … and don't let this be called my death bed. Rather, let it be called my bed of life and take my body from it to help others lead fuller lives.

Give my sight to the man who has never seen a sunrise, a baby's face, or love in the eyes of a woman. Give my heart to a person whose own heart has caused nothing but endless days of pain. Give my blood to the teenager who was pulled from the wreckage of his car so that he might live to see his grandchildren play. Give my kidneys to one who depends upon a machine to exist. Take my bones, every muscle, every nerve, every fiber in my body and find a way to make a crippled child walk. Explore every corner of my brain, take my cells if necessary, and let them grow so that someday a speechless boy will shout at the crack of a bat, and a deaf girl will hear the sound of rain against her window. Burn what is left of me and scatter the ashes to the four winds to help flowers grow.

If you must bury something, let it be my faults, my weaknesses and all my prejudice against my fellow man. If, by chance, you do wish to remember me, do it with a kind word or deed to someone who needs you.

If you do all that I have asked, I will live forever.

Robert Noel Test

To order additional copies of:

Book: If All Else Fails ... Laugh!

Audio book on CD: If All Else Fails ... Laugh

Six CD set: Laugh, Live and Learn

Phone: 830-997-9721
or visit:
www.suziehumphreys.com

To contact Suzie about her speaking presentations
Phone: 830-997-9721
or
E-mail: suzie@ctesc.net